of the Golden Scepter

Lois T. Henderson

Scripture Union
130 City Road London EC1V 2NJ

Touch of the Golden Scepter

Published in the USA by David C. Cook Publishing Co., Elgin, Il 60120

Published in the UK by Scripture Union, 1983
Reprinted 1984
ISBN 0 85421 995 1

Printed in Great Britain by
Ebenezer Baylis and Son Limited,
The Trinity Press, Worcester, and London.

ON TRIAL . . .

The number on Hadassah's token was called, and in a moment she felt herself being pushed into the silken tent where the king's officials were selecting girls to compete to be queen.

"Can you believe it?" said one man's voice. "Here's the first one whose face we won't have to wash."

"That will save us some time," said another. "Open your mouth, girl."

Furious, Hadassah did as she was told.

"Her teeth are good. Skin clear. Hair thick . . . "

The evaluation was made in a bored voice, and Hadassah felt that the eyes that examined her so closely somehow did not see *her* at all. . . .

Dedicated to
Beth and Joshua
Rachel and John
with my love

Author's Note

Although I have been true in this book to the basic story of Esther as it appears in the Old Testament, I have also allowed my imagination to fill in the background when the Bible is silent. For example, the Bible records only that Esther was an orphan. In the early chapters I've given an imaginary tale explaining how that might have come about.

Esther's Hebrew name was Hadassah. Esther, the Persian name, was not given to her until she entered the court.

King Ahasuerus is referred to in history and in some Bible translations as King Xerxes I of Persia, but in this book I have used the traditional Bible name for him.

The Bible calls Haman an "Agagite." Some Bible scholars believe this meant he was an Amalekite, related to the Amalekite king, Agag.

The story's action begins at about the year 485 B.C.

Lois Henderson
Coraopolis, Pennsylvania

Contents

1

Night Attack

The light from the fire threw red and gold streamers against the dark night sky. Hadassah, weary from the long days of travel, almost envied her younger sister, who lay with her head on their mother's lap. At twelve, Hadassah was much too old to put her head on someone's lap. But oh, wouldn't it be lovely to rest on that soft, safe pillow, sheltered from the dark desert night that stretched so huge around them?

"Hadassah, are you listening?"

Her father's voice jerked her away from her thoughts.

"Yes, father. . . . Well, truthfully, I'm not listening as closely as I should," she apologized. "I'm so tired. We've walked so far in these past few days."

"I know." Her father nodded. "We are almost done walking. But now I have something important to explain. You've got to listen."

Hadassah wished that whatever he had to tell her could wait until morning. All she wanted to do was sleep.

"I wish we could have stayed in Babylon," she murmured. "It's the only place I ever remember living. My friends were there—Miriam and Rachel. Why do we have to go to Shushan? What's there that we didn't have in Babylon?"

"You know Babylon is not our own land." There was a thread of irritation in her father's voice, so Hadassah forced herself to pay attention. "You've heard the stories many times of how Nebuchadnezzar came to Israel, and captured the people, and scattered us—our people, that is—to all the parts of the earth. It was the fate of our family to end up in Babylon."

"Fate?" Hadassah thought of their comfortable house, of her friends, of the marvelous buildings and gardens of the city itself.

"It was a foreign place," her father said, a stubborn note creeping into his voice. "For us Jews, there is no real home except Israel. I've told you that ever since you were a baby."

"Yes, father." She was starting to get sleepy again.

"Not that you can understand, I suppose. You're too young. But this journey—it's a dangerous one, and we might—well, we could even be separated."

"You should have told her before." Hadassah's mother sounded tired, too.

"But I didn't," he said. "So, now, Hadassah, listen.

Wherever we go, whatever happens, don't ever forget that you're a Jew. And Jews have enemies. Sometimes I think the whole world is our enemy. We've been killed for no other reason than that we worship our God, Yahweh,* and no other god. You *must* understand this."

Something about his voice brought Hadassah awake. "Is that what was going to happen in Babylon?" she asked in a small voice. Surely there had not been any enemies in Babylon. She couldn't remember a single act or word of anger.

Her father shrugged. "We don't know. There were rumors. There are always rumors, it's true. But this time there seemed to be more reason to believe them. And when we received a letter from my nephew, Mordecai, telling us how things were in the city of Shushan, we decided to go there."

"Well, I knew we were going to live with *some* relative," Hadassah said, hoping this was the end of her father's speech.

"Listen," her father said firmly. "His name is Mordecai. Can you remember that?"

"Of course. Mordecai. Why do I have to remember?"

"That's what I'm trying to tell you. We're coming to a dangerous part of the journey. Thieves hide in these mountain passes and attack small caravans like this one. So you must know—in case we should be separated."

A tiny touch of fear moved coldly through Hadassah.

"His name is Mordecai," her father said. "And he

---

*Yahweh was the Israelites' name for God.

lives on the Street of Poppies. He's a gatekeeper for the king, so almost anyone would know him. Can you remember that?"

"His name is Mordecai," Hadassah said slowly, as though reciting a lesson. "He lives on the Street of Poppies, and he's a gatekeeper for the king. You don't have to worry. I won't forget."

"And don't forget that—" her father began, but her mother interrupted.

"You'll frighten her with all this talk. Come, Hadassah," she urged. "Come and lie down here beside your sister. Try to get some sleep. We have another two days of walking before we get to Shushan."

Hadassah moved over and curled up on the mat beside her younger sister. How good it felt to close her eyes against the light of the fire, to shut her mind to the sound of voices.

But just before she slept, she heard her mother ask, "Did it really look like a band of Amalekites?"

The first words of her father's answer were blurred by Hadassah's sleepiness. But she swam up out of unconsciousness in time to hear him say, "Joash recognized the weapons and the clothes they wore. What's more, the Amalekites could probably tell that this caravan was made up mostly of Jews. They could easily come back this way and attack us."

"Oh, surely not, Abihail," Hadassah's mother began. Her voice was so comfortable and unalarmed that Hadassah allowed herself to sink back into the safe, untroubled world of sleep.

The word that woke her up was the very same word she had heard her father and mother whispering before she had drifted off to sleep.

"Amalekites!" the sentry screamed.

Or was she only dreaming? Had her father's fear become the topic of a nightmare, perhaps?

Someone running stumbled over Hadassah, and she felt the shock of a bare foot painfully in the small of her back. This was no dream. She sat up and almost immediately heard her father's voice.

"Hadassah, run! Run toward those gullies, the ones we passed last night. Try not to fall. As soon as you're out of the firelight, get down on your knees and crawl. Keep yourself hidden. We'll catch up to you. Now, run!"

Hadassah saw him shaking her sister, saw him turn urgently to her mother. Then she ran in the direction his finger had pointed.

Already she could hear screams and moans—and savage shouts of glee. She ran in a black terror, bruising her feet against stones, falling to her knees, trying to run again. She turned and saw her father against the light of the fire. Her mother had tripped and fallen, and he was stooping over her.

Behind them a huge figure approached, roaring, wheeling his sword in wicked arcs.

For an instant, Hadassah hesitated. Part of her wanted to go back, to do something. . . . But another part of her took control, turned her face away from the scene of horror and carried her—crawling, panting, blind—out of the circle of light and into the darkness.

Every minute she expected a sword to impale her. She had no hope of survival. She kept going only because that was what her father had told her to do.

Suddenly footsteps sounded behind her, and she

tried to flatten herself against the ground. But then the earth seemed to open up under her. She fell, sprawling, into a sort of pit, striking her head against a stone, and slid into oblivion.

When she woke up, the world was silent again, and day was growing along the distant hills.

I dreamed it all, Hadassah thought. Then she tried to move. Pain hit her at the same time she realized that she was not on a mat by the fire but lying, twisted, on a ledge of stone. *Then it* was *real*, she thought.

I've got to go back and get them, she said to herself. *I've got to find them.* She would not let the vision of that sword, whirling, red in the firelight, enter her mind.

Climbing up out of the gully was not difficult. She had not been seriously hurt when she had fallen, and the roughness of the ground provided toeholds and fingerholds for her so that she was able to scramble up to the path from which she'd fallen.

It never occurred to her to try to hide. If her father and mother were alive, she had no need to hide. And if they were not alive, why should she shelter herself?

As she stumbled down the path, the ruined camp appeared suddenly before her. A half-dozen people wandered around aimlessly, their weeping making a thin, mournful sound in the morning air. It was obvious that the Amalekites were gone.

A woman caught sight of Hadassah approaching. "Ah, praise to our God, another one. Look, Aaron, it's Hadassah. She's alive!"

Hadassah recognized the woman who ran toward

her as one named Leah. When they came together, Leah embraced her so tightly that it hurt Hadassah's ribs. Then she stood back and looked at Hadassah.

"You're all right!" Leah exclaimed. "They didn't hurt you?"

Hadassah didn't bother to answer. "What about my father?" she burst out. "My mother—my sister?"

Leah shook her head. "Come," she said, holding out a hand, "come with me over here by the fire. It's better that you don't look."

Hadassah pushed the hand away. Last night she had run in terror, as a coward would run. *I will never run away again*, she thought with shame.

She wandered alone through the camp, staring in silence at the bodies all around her, stiffened into strange positions in death. When she found her parents and sister, she made no sound. It was like a dream: Their white faces, the red-brown blood, their blank, staring eyes somehow did not seem to affect her. She felt as dead as they. It was only later, as Leah forced her to drink a little wine, that the tears gushed out in a torrent of pain.

When Leah and the other surviving members of the caravan decided to find a village that would take them in and supply them with donkeys, so they could reach Shushan, Hadassah went with them obediently.

It wasn't right. She knew it wasn't right. They should stay here longer and bury the bodies of their people. But terror had made the adults unreasonable, and who would listen to a child?

Before they got too far away, she turned and saw again where the bodies of her parents and her sister were huddled on the sand.

Someday, she promised, shaping the words inside herself, *someday I'll make it up to you. I swear it!*

She was in too much shock to understand what she had just promised. She only knew that a flame of hate had begun to burn in her, and all her tears could not put it out.

2

Uncle Mordecai

"Mordecai? On the Street of Poppies?" The gatekeeper at the main entrance to Shushan wrinkled his forehead. "Oh, yes, of course. Mordecai. I don't know him personally, but I know who you mean."

Hadassah, standing behind Leah, drooping with grief and fatigue, wished the man would get on with it. *If he would talk less and point more,* she thought bitterly, *we might find this cousin of mine more easily.*

"The Street of Poppies is only four streets over," the gatekeeper informed the travelers. "It runs east and west, just as this street in front of you. See where the mosaic ends? Go to that corner. Turn left and go along until you come to . . . Let's see, how can I explain it?"

"I should think we could count four streets," Hadassah said in the brittle voice that she had used since the night of the tragedy. She had found that only anger could keep her from weeping endlessly.

The man peered beyond Leah and stared at Hadassah. "A rude snip of a girl," he observed. "Is her tongue always so pointed?"

Leah made a small sound of distress. "The child's whole family was killed recently in—an accident," she said hastily. "She is still in a shocked condition."

"Well, children are expected to be obedient here," the man pointed out. "She'd do well to watch what she says. But she's right, of course. You can count four streets. There are paths and byways that might confuse you, but let *her* count. She'll be able to tell you."

Hadassah looked at him with no change of expression.

The gatekeeper's eyes finally moved from hers. "And there's a grove of olive trees on the corner of the Street of Poppies," he remembered. "Mordecai's house is about halfway down the street. You'll have to ask."

"Thank you." Leah nudged Hadassah, reminding her of her manners.

"Thank you," Hadassah repeated mechanically.

"It's nothing!" The gatekeeper responded, suddenly smiling with a great show of warmth. "Go in peace."

Leading the ragged donkeys they had purchased from some friendly villagers with their only money, the coins which had been sewn into Leah's robe, the small party of Jews moved slowly along the streets of Shushan. They had apparently come into the city's market area, for small shops and booths lined both sides of the street. In one, Hadassah saw great piles of melons glowing on the shelves. In another there were trays of crisp-crusted, braided bread.

For the first time in days, Hadassah felt a slight twinge of hunger. Perhaps the security of the busy street was making her feel more normal. All during the last part of the journey through the wilderness she had walked in fear, expecting a steel blade between her shoulders with every step she took. Here she finally felt safe.

"It looks a little like home," she ventured to Leah.

"Home? Oh, you mean Babylon. Yes, it does a little. This is supposed to be a rich city. The king of Persia has his grandest palace here, so we'll see sights as marvelous as Babylon's, I suppose."

Hadassah lapsed back into silence. They walked on, and in a few minutes Hadassah pointed mutely to a grove of olive trees. Leah nodded and led the way down the road that was called the Street of Poppies.

The houses were small, but clean and sturdy. *This must be where the merchants live, merchants and scholars and gatekeepers*, Hadassah thought. She was remembering her father's words, "A gatekeeper for the king."

Had things been different, she would have been curious about what the king's gatekeeper did. And she would have been wondering what Mordecai was like—and even if he would want to be responsible for her, now that she had come alone. But the dark, hollow pain that filled her left no room for any of her normal thoughts.

"Tell me," Leah called to a woman who was hanging

a rug out over a second-story balcony, "is the house of Mordecai on this street? Do you know where he lives?"

The woman leaned over the balcony to stare down at them. "You must be his relatives from Babylon," she shouted. "He's been looking for you for days. Half-crazy with worry. Like a woman he's been, cleaning and fretting."

Leah kept her voice patient and Hadassah stared at the ground. "His house is where, then?" Leah asked.

The woman pointed. "That one. See, with the vine climbing over the door? He's home. I saw him only a few minutes ago."

"Thank you," Leah said and turned away.

But the woman leaned even more precariously over the balcony. "Are you Hadassah?" she called, and Hadassah could not keep from looking up at the sound of her name.

"My daughter Rebekkah is just your age," the woman said, smiling. "She's been looking forward to your coming, ever since Mordecai told us."

This time Hadassah didn't need Leah's prodding. "Thank you," she said gratefully.

In just a few minutes Leah was knocking on Mordecai's door. At once there was the sound of someone hurrying toward it.

Hadassah found herself staring apprehensively at the door. *What if—*

She had no time to shape her worry into words. Mordecai, his robe flying, his dark hair and beard blowing back as though he were running, came striding out of the door.

His hands were stretched out in welcome, and he

was crying, "My Uncle Abihail!" before he even saw them. Then he stopped and gazed at them blankly, astonished at having a woman at his door. He looked beyond Leah, beyond Hadassah, and then saw the men who stood holding the donkeys' ropes.

"I am expecting my uncle," Mordecai explained, still looking bewildered. "When I saw travelers—"

Leah pushed Hadassah toward him. "This is your cousin, Hadassah," she said loudly, uncomfortably. "Her parents—"

Hadassah interrupted. "My parents were killed by a band of Amalekites," she said in her new, brittle voice.

Mordecai looked at her, stunned. His large eyes filled with tears. "What did you say?" he asked, his voice shaking.

But Hadassah could not repeat those terrible words. She stood staring up into the face of the tall man. His eyes with their heavy lashes, now brilliant with tears, were like her father's eyes.

Leah broke the silence. "She spoke truly, sir. Her parents, as well as many others—my husband among them—were killed two days' journey away. We've brought you the child."

A look of panic flitted across Mordecai's face. Hadassah could imagine the thought that must have raced through his mind. *A child? To me?* But almost instantly the panic was pushed aside.

"And why not?" he cried. "My own cousin. Where else should she go? Especially now that her father—" His words came to an abrupt halt. He opened his arms, and in just a second, Hadassah was held awkwardly in a large, warm embrace.

At his touch, all her brittle strength deserted her, and she was clinging, sobbing, burrowing her head against the coarse robe.

Mordecai held her, murmuring the small, foolish words one says to a baby. "There, there. It's all right now. It's all right."

In Mordecai's arms, strangely enough, Hadassah felt the pain of her loss more sharply than she had felt it yet. At the same time, her cousin's arms seemed to be a shelter against the cold that had filled her mind and heart.

Leah watched them a few minutes in silence, and then she spoke. "We'll leave you, then."

Mordecai looked up. His face was wet with tears, and he seemed confused. "I'm sorry. Come in, please. Let me give you food. May I offer you a place to stay? Please—I'm sorry."

Leah's hands brushed away his apology. "No, never mind. We have homes of relatives to find, all five of us. We thought it was best to get the small one settled first. She has no belongings."

"But she's alive," Mordecai said, and Hadassah heard the sincere gratitude in his words. "I'll find clothes for her. I'm not rich, but we'll manage. She'll be—if she's willing, that is—the daughter I never had."

Hadassah was weak from crying, so she clung to her cousin's arm as she turned to Leah.

"Thank you," she said. Her voice was no longer harsh and brittle. "Thank you . . . for taking care of me."

Leah's eyes brimmed. "It has been a joy to see you safely home."

Hadassah tried to smile. What had her father said—

that there was no real home except Israel? Well, for her, there was no real home anywhere.

"Will I see you sometime?" Hadassah asked.

"Yes, surely," Leah answered. "I know where you are, and I'll come to see you after we're settled." She reached over and hugged the girl. "Yahweh surely has a task for you to do," she whispered. "For all of us. Why else were we saved from slaughter?"

Hadassah nodded against Leah's shoulder. She felt a momentary urge to cry out that she didn't really want to be alive, but she didn't trust her voice. Besides, it might distress this gentle man who had welcomed her. She didn't want him to think badly of her.

"Then, we had better get about doing whatever it is we have to do." Leah made her voice firm as she stood back from Hadassah. "First, I must find my family. And you, you must be a good daughter to your cousin."

"I'll try," Hadassah promised and stood with Mordecai to watch the others trudge away.

When they were gone, Mordecai turned to Hadassah. "Come in," he said. "Are you hungry? Thirsty? Would you like to wash?"

She followed him into the house but was unable to see anything at first because her eyes were still accustomed to the sun. "Perhaps I might wash," she suggested. "I know I must be dirty." Her voice wavered on the edge of a sob. "Then, if you don't mind, I saw some bread at the market as we came into town, and it made me hungry. I—I haven't eaten since—"

"I went to the market this morning as my wife used to," Mordecai said quickly. "I have bread and goat's cheese . . . I'll show you the room where you can wash.

It will be your room now."

He led her through a narrow door into a tiny room. She saw four mats rolled up against the wall and knew the room was to have been for her whole family.

Mordecai picked up the extra mats without a word. "There's water in the jar," he said. "I'll go out and fix the food."

"Thank you," she said, grateful for his understanding. "May I call you Uncle Mordecai? You seem too old to be a cousin."

Her eyes were getting used to the dimness, so she saw the smile that lit up his face. "By all means, call me uncle. My father was years older than your father, so I am nearly your father's age. I've been a widower for several years, and we had no children. I would be proud to have you call me uncle."

He turned to leave the room.

"Uncle Mordecai," she called softly, and he paused at the door. "Tomorrow *I'll* go to the market. You needn't be a housewife now that I'm here to help."

She had wondered if she could ever smile again, but at Mordecai's look of delight, she found her lips curving up of their own accord. She and Mordecai looked at each other for a minute, both of them smiling, with the marks of tears still on their cheeks.

"So, wash now," Mordecai said in a father's voice, and she turned from him to pour water into a shallow basin. Perhaps, in this house, she thought, she could learn to live again.

3

A Forbidden Glimpse

There was no sound in the quiet house except the soft clicking of Hadassah's clay spindle. She had become so expert in the twisting of the fibers to make yarn that she could do it without looking. Uncle Mordecai had fixed a tilted rack that could hold a scroll and still leave her hands free. As a result, she could spin and read at the same time.

A noise at the door made her look up, but she felt no sense of alarm. The nightmares she'd had so often when she had first come to live in Shushan two years ago were now things of the past. She no longer lived with the fear that danger lurked in every shadow and loud noise.

Rebekkah stood in the doorway, peering uncertainly into the dim room. "Hadassah," she called. "Are you there?"

"Yes, over here by the window. Just wait until your eyes are used to being inside, and then come and sit by me."

Rebekkah groped her way impatiently across the room. "Don't tell me you're reading again," she cried with disgust. "You're not a man, you know, not a scholar. Why your uncle taught you to read, I'll never understand."

Hadassah laughed at her friend. "You're just jealous. I've told you a hundred times: Uncle Mordecai would teach a pigeon how to read. He's just a natural teacher."

Rebekkah shook her head in irritation. "Women don't need to read. And, besides, those dry old scrolls could never be as exciting as the news I heard today."

"What?—a new caravan has come to town, with silk from the east?"

Rebekkah plopped onto a stool and glared at Hadassah. "You always make fun of me," she pouted. "Can I help it if I like pretty things?"

"No, of course not. Any more than I can help liking to read. But is that it? A new caravan?"

"No. Something far more exciting than that. It has to do with Queen Vashti."

"She hasn't had a child, has she?" Hadassah asked.

"Not that one," Rebekkah said, but she cast a quick look over her shoulder to be sure that no one was listening. "She cares only about being beautiful and making all the wives of the visiting officials jealous by showing off the riches of her palace. Surely your uncle has told you about the marvelous feast that's being held?"

Hadassah nodded. "Yes, of course. It seems as if they've been having it forever. Wasn't last night the seventh night? You'd think they'd all have indigestion."

Rebekkah giggled. "You hadn't better let anyone hear you say that. How could anyone get indigestion from *royal* food?"

"The same way I get it from unroyal food. By eating too much."

Rebekkah lowered her voice. "I imagine Queen Vashti wishes she had something as ordinary as indigestion to worry about."

Hadassah felt the first real quickening of interest. "Is there trouble at the palace? And, anyway, how do you know?"

"Well," Rebekkah began, and then suddenly her eyes widened. "You mean your uncle hasn't told you?"

Hadassah gave her a small push. She knew exactly what Rebekkah meant. Every time she tried to tell Hadassah something important, Hadassah already knew about it. *I can't help it*, Hadassah reminded herself, *that Uncle Mordecai is the palace gatekeeper and tells me everything.*

For a few seconds, Hadassah's mind skittered over the past two years, over the warm, delightful friendship that had grown up between the lonely man and the bereaved child. Probably no two people had ever needed each other more. He was father, mother, and brother to her, and she tried to be both daughter and son to him.

"A shocking thing," Rebekkah was saying, watching

to see that her friend was listening. Hadassah blinked and focused on the conversation again. "Last night," Rebekkah continued, "the king commanded Queen Vashti to appear before all his guests, and she refused! Just flatly refused."

Hadassah stared at her. "But no one refuses King Ahasuerus anything."

"I know. Or—off with his head! Or in this case, *her* head. But she did refuse him."

"Did he cut off her head?" Hadassah's eyes were wide with horror, and for just an instant she saw the wicked sword, red in the firelight, whirling and plunging.

"No, of course not. I was just saying that. But he was angry. Very, very angry."

Hadassah sat for a minute, thinking of the king's anger. He had absolute power, she knew, and could decide whether anyone would live or die. *I just hope he never gets mad at the Jews,* Hadassah thought, and wondered if she dared share the idea even with Rebekkah. She decided she'd better not.

"So what did he do?" Hadassah's voice was as anxious and breathless as Rebekkah could have wanted. "And you've never even told me where you heard this."

"Everyone knows," Rebekkah said with a sweeping gesture. "My father heard the men talking about it as they came into his shop. And my mother said women were talking about it in the market."

Hadassah slowly put down her spindle. "I don't understand," she began.

"She did it publicly," Rebekkah informed her. "Well, actually he commanded her to appear publicly, and she sent back word that she would not. Can you imagine what that must have been like?"

Hadassah was silent, her mind working furiously. She was thinking of the one time she had seen King Ahasuerus. She had gone to the market for food, and the royal carriage had thundered by, dust flying from the horses' swift feet. As the carriage swept past, the wind had blown the curtains aside and she had had one quick glimpse of the interior. A young man sat there in splendid isolation on scarlet and gold cushions. He was incredibly handsome, with black curls spilling onto his forehead, blazing black eyes, and olive skin.

She had been terrified rather than thrilled. Common people were not supposed to see the king's face, and she had glanced around quickly to see if anyone on the street was watching her.

In spite of her fear, she had noticed the expression on his face. The young monarch's mouth had drooped with what was obviously boredom or unhappiness. One question had haunted her ever since: How could anyone be king of Persia and not be happy?

Hadassah brought her wandering mind back to the present. Rebekkah was saying, "The men were simply furious. They said if the queen refused to obey the king, wouldn't every wife in the land feel she could refuse to obey her husband?"

Unexpectedly, Hadassah began to laugh. "Can't you just picture some of the timid little wives on this street refusing to obey their husbands?"

Rebekkah didn't even smile. "It's serious," she insisted. "I mean, it's really serious. I don't see how you can laugh."

Hadassah made her face sober. "So what happened? What did he do to her?"

"Nothing, yet," Rebekkah admitted. "Some people say she'll be killed. Others say she'll be sent back to her home, which is the most humiliating thing he could do to her. There are a hundred stories, all of them different."

"I'd like to see the palace just once," Hadassah commented. "Uncle Mordecai says there are pillars of marble, and that some of the furniture is actually made of gold."

"Why not? After all, he's king over all the lands from India to Ethiopia."

Hadassah's mind tried to visualize such an empire, but it was too vast. "Just to be king of Shushan ought to be grand enough," she murmured.

"King Ahasuerus would laugh at that," Rebekkah said scornfully.

"He's probably not laughing today," Hadassah said. "I wonder if he loved her."

"Who?"

"Why, Queen Vashti, of course. Who else?"

It was obviously a new idea to Rebekkah. She stared at Hadassah. "What difference would that make?" she asked blankly.

Hadassah felt a thrust of impatience. "Why, all the difference in the world, silly. Can you imagine what it would be like for him to love her and yet have to do something terrible to her?"

Rebekkah stared in astonishment, her mouth slightly agape, then apparently decided to change the subject. "Why hasn't he ever taken you to the palace?"

"King Ahasuerus?"

Rebekkah giggled. "No, of course not. Your uncle. He's a gatekeeper for the king. Surely he could take you to the palace if he wanted to."

Hadassah shook her head. "It's not wise."

"Why not?"

"We're not Persians," Hadassah offered.

"Well, of course not, we're Jews. What difference does that make?"

Hadassah stared at her friend. Sometimes she thought that Rebekkah was one of the nicest things that had happened to her in Shushan, but sometimes she wanted to shake her.

"Being a Jew can cause you a lot of trouble," she said flatly. "Haven't your parents warned you not to talk about it?"

"Well, of course. It's never smart to boast that you weren't born a Persian. But surely there's no danger."

Hadassah bit her lip and looked down. With a slow, deliberate movement, she picked up her spindle again. "I really must do my work," she said. "I have to finish this spinning, and then get the food ready for our supper. Uncle Mordecai will be home before dark."

Rebekkah looked miserable. "I'm sorry," she said. "I didn't even think. Of course you know all about danger and what can happen to Jews. I'm sorry."

"It's all right," Hadassah said.

Rebekkah sat quietly a minute and then got up. "I always talk too much. . . . You know how I am. But—I'm sorry."

Hadassah made her voice cheerful. "Well, I'm glad you *do* talk, or how else would I hear the gossip about the queen?"

Rebekkah looked relieved. "I'll tell you more if I hear anything," she promised. "And if your uncle tells you, you're to tell me. All right?"

Hadassah nodded. "Yes, fine. I'll see you in the morning when we go for water."

Rebekkah ran out with a quick wave. For a few minutes Hadassah sat engulfed in a bleak misery, and then she resolutely put it from her mind.

When Uncle Mordecai comes home, she thought, *I'll ask him about Queen Vashti. She can't be too much older than I am. They haven't been married long.*

The memory of her glimpse of King Ahasuerus sitting in his carriage flitted across her mind again. *Surely if he had loved Vashti, he wouldn't have looked so dissatisfied with life,* Hadassah thought. *My mother and father made each other happy.*

She recalled the evenings in Babylon, when her father had come home from his little shop. She could still remember the way he smiled at her mother, and how much they enjoyed talking together. Hadassah had taken the love they had for each other for granted then. Now she knew that love did not always dwell in the marriages parents arranged for their children.

With a pleasant shiver, she remembered the words of a song King Solomon had written in one of Uncle Mordecai's scrolls of Jewish Scripture:

"Love burns like blazing fire,
  like a mighty flame.
Many waters cannot quench love;
  rivers cannot wash it away.
If one were to give all the wealth of his house for love,
  it would be utterly scorned."

The sun sank lower in the sky, and the shadows in the Street of Poppies grew long. With a start, Hadassah came out of her reverie. Uncle Mordecai would be home soon.

If I read fast, she thought, *I can finish this section of this history scroll before I have to start cooking.* Her fingers flew on the clay spindle, and her eyes devoured the lettering as fast as possible. In only a minute, she was totally absorbed in her reading and her spinning. She had completely forgotten about love songs and the disobedient queen.

4

King without a Queen

If Rebekkah thinks my reading is shocking, Hadassah thought, reaching for a wedge of bread, *what would she think if she knew Uncle Mordecai and I eat together?* Although men and women did not normally eat together, Uncle Mordecai had insisted that they share their evening meal ever since she had come to Shushan.

"How foolish for me to eat in loneliness and you to eat in loneliness," he had said. "We might as well talk a little while we eat."

So now it had become a habit, and some of their best conversations were shared over food.

"Uncle Mordecai," Hadassah said suddenly, "I want to ask you something."

"Of course, my child. What?"

"Well, Rebekkah was here today. You know how she always has something to talk about. Today she was telling some unbelievable story about Queen Vashti. I was just wondering if it were true."

Mordecai's face showed a mixture of pity and worry. "What did she tell you?" His voice was cautious.

"She said the queen had disobeyed her husband and had refused to appear before his guests." Like Rebekkah, Hadassah spoke quietly so no one outside would hear her.

Mordecai lowered his voice. "Well, yes, it's true. It all happened after I left my post last night, but everyone's talking about it. The king—well, he must have been drunk to ask his wife, the queen of the land, to parade in front of his guests, like a—a common dancer. She was insulted and angry, I'm told."

"But to refuse him!" Hadassah protested. "He could have her beheaded."

"Or hung on a gibbet," Mordecai agreed. "I don't think he will, though."

"Why not?"

"Because I don't think he's a cruel man. He's young, and he's foolish, perhaps overly proud of his possessions. But not cruel."

"Especially if he loves her," Hadassah said.

Mordecai pushed back his bowl and took several dates from a dish in the center of the mat. "I'm not at all sure that he loves her. She's very beautiful, but I've been told that she has a vicious tongue. Even her husband was not safe from her sharp remarks, they say."

"Well, if he has to kill her or send her back to her

father," Hadassah said, "it's better if he doesn't love her. Then he won't even care."

"Oh, he'll care," Mordecai argued. "He'll care because he has been humiliated in front of many important men. I wouldn't want to be in her place."

"Nor I." Hadassah took a few of the dates, too. "But, then, we Jews don't have kings and queens with power like that."

"Nor a free land of our own for them to rule," Mordecai mourned. "At least, we who are scattered over the face of the earth don't have our own land. But someday . . ."

It was a hope he expressed constantly, almost like a prayer, so that Hadassah hardly heard it any more.

"What will he do, do you think?" she asked, ignoring Mordecai's last remark. "King Ahasuerus, I mean."

Mordecai shrugged. "What can a man do in such a circumstance? He'll send her away, probably, and he'll tell the whole world that women mean nothing to him, and that he doesn't care a fig about what has happened. And then, after a while, he'll get lonely and he'll get his highest ministers, the emirs, to begin to look for a queen—a beautiful, intelligent, and *humble* queen."

Hadassah's eyes sparkled. "Is it possible to be beautiful, intelligent, and humble, Uncle Mordecai? How can anyone be humble if she is both beautiful and intelligent?"

Mordecai looked at Hadassah for a long, silent moment, and then he answered in a very solemn voice. "You should know. You do it."

"Do what?"

"You manage to be humble, in spite of your beauty

and your intelligence, my daughter."

She stared at him, and then her head tipped back and laughter bubbled out of her. "Oh, Uncle Mordecai, you're teasing me again."

But his voice was completely serious. "I'm not. It's a new idea to me, too, I'll admit. I know you're intelligent, and you don't put on airs. But I hadn't realized how beautiful you are."

She felt the warmth of her blood in her cheeks. "You're joking," she mumbled. "I'm not beautiful. And besides, you're always telling me that proverb from the Scriptures: 'Charm is deceptive, and beauty is fleeting, but a woman who fears Yahweh is to be praised.' "

He smiled. "Such a sharp memory! But the man who wrote that didn't mean there was anything wrong with beauty, Hadassah. He meant that the fear of Yahweh brings a beauty of soul that lasts far longer than other beauty. But, anyway, little one, how do you know what you look like? Do we have a metal mirror like the queen's to see your face in?"

"Well, no," she admitted. "But I've—I've seen my face in water."

Mordecai laughed. "Moving water, so that your mouth would run sideways up one cheek and your eyes would come together over your nose."

Hadassah giggled. "But it would give me *some* idea."

"Tell me," he said abruptly, "do you remember how lovely your mother was?"

Her heart seemed to be squeezed with pain. "Yes," she whispered, "I remember."

"Well, you're lovelier," he said gently. "Your eyes are like your father's: large, dark, and with long lashes.

Your mother's eyes were not so beautiful."

"Then my eyes are like yours," Hadassah said, looking affectionately at the man facing her. His hair was starting to grow gray, and there were small lines in his face, but his eyes were bright and clear.

"Yes. We inherit them from our grandmother. But you have your mother's nose, straight and narrow, and her lovely mouth. I don't have to tell you what your hair is like. You see how black and thick and wavy it is every time you brush it or oil it or braid it."

"It's possible that you only see me that way because you—like me."

Mordecai laughed again. "Because I love you, you mean," he insisted. "But you're wrong. If I loved you less, I might have seen your beauty sooner. I've been looking at you with a father's eyes, seeing only a little girl. I hadn't realized you were grown up." His voice was sad.

"I'm fourteen," she reminded him.

"I know. Old enough for marriage. I hadn't realized."

"I don't plan to get married, if you don't mind." Her voice was anxious. "I'd rather stay with you, and keep house, and read, and just do as I've been doing. I don't have to get married right away, do I?"

He tried to smile. "You won't be considered an old maid until you're eighteen, I suppose. But a good father tries to arrange a proper marriage for a daughter before she's sixteen, at least."

"Then give me another year before you even start thinking about it," she begged. "Please, Uncle Mordecai, I—I don't want to leave you."

"Rebekkah's father is making marriage arrangements for her," Mordecai reminded her. "Doesn't that mean anything to you?"

"Well, of course. It means that Rebekkah will move away, but not far away. Joakim is the boy they've chosen, and you know he only lives down the street. Rebekkah will go to his parents' house to live, but I'll still see her at the well each day. We'll still be friends."

Mordecai shook his head. "Marriage means more than just moving to another house. It means she'll have babies, and she'll be spending her time with her children and working for her mother-in-law. It won't be the same."

Hadassah got up abruptly and began to stack the bowls together. "That may all be true, but it doesn't change how I feel. Can't I have another year with you, Uncle Mordecai?"

His eyes were soft. "I can't promise, little one. I know I'll grieve worse than any mother when you leave me. But what if some rich, handsome son of a merchant comes to my door—or his father does, I mean—and asks for you? Could I refuse?"

She tried to smile, knowing he wasn't wholly serious. "No," she admitted, "I don't suppose you could."

"Or King Ahasuerus," Mordecai went on, his eyes sparkling now. "That's a thought. What if the king would ride by in his chariot and see you sweeping the yard? And what if he would say, 'There is the girl I need to put on my throne'? Would you have me say, 'I'm sorry, my lord, but she will not leave her old uncle'?"

Hadassah's laughter spilled out in a silver waterfall of sound. "No, in that case, I think you should say,

'Well, my lord, if you'll give her books to read and if you'll give her permission to come home to visit every other week, I'll let her go.' "

"Or, better yet," Mordecai said, entering into the game, "I'll say, 'You may have her, my lord, if you make me ruling emir over half your kingdom.' How would that be?"

They laughed and Hadassah got up to carry the dishes away.

The days slid by, and to Hadassah's immense relief, there was no further talk of marriage for her. She and her cousin talked about the scrolls they read. During the hours Mordecai was at the palace, Hadassah spun yarn and ground grain, kneaded bread and gathered olives to be put down in oil, wove cloth, and carried water. And she was happy.

Then one day Mordecai burst through the doorway with a blaze of excitement in his face.

"You look as though someone just gave you a bushel of gold," Hadassah greeted him.

"It's possible," Mordecai answered.

"What do you mean?"

"Well, not gold, of course. But the possibility of riches. Riches beyond your imagining."

"Are you teasing again?" she asked suspiciously.

"No, listen. The king has decided to take another queen. Just as I predicted he would. An edict has been sent out that all the most beautiful girls in the land are to be gathered together. Then they're to be sorted out according to beauty and brains and breeding—"

"Like cattle," Hadassah interrupted rudely.

Mordecai ignored her. "And the loveliest and wisest of them will be kept in the palace for a year to be trained in all manner of things. Then they will meet the king, and he will choose the most beautiful of all."

"To be queen?" Her voice went high with astonishment.

"To be queen. To sit by his side and share with him in the ruling of his kingdom."

"Oh, come now, Uncle Mordecai," Hadassah said bluntly. "What woman shares in the ruling of anything?"

"There is no limit to the suggestions a woman can make—if she is careful enough—that a man who loves her will carry out for her."

Hadassah grew sober. "A spiteful queen could harm a whole kingdom, then. And a good and loving queen could . . ."

Mordecai's voice was soft but shaking with excitement. "Exactly, my child. Exactly. And I believe—I *know*—that you can be such a queen."

"Me?" Hadassah gasped. "But I'm only a Jewish orphan."

"But no one needs to know that you're a Jew," Mordecai said. "And if you're an orphan, what of that? With Yahweh's help, I believe you can be queen of Persia."

Hadassah began to laugh, but the sound caught unexpectedly on a sob, and throwing herself in Mordecai's arms, she burst into tears.

5

Kohl for the Eyes

"If I were you, I'd be thrilled!" Rebekkah, her water jar balanced on her shoulder, looked at Hadassah with astonishment. "Why do you think it will be so terrible?"

Hadassah kicked viciously at a pebble and was rewarded with a sharp pain in her toe. *Sandals were never meant to protect anything but the soles of one's feet*, she reflected sourly. She finally turned to Rebekkah. "What's so wonderful about being herded with a hundred other girls through a dozen humiliating tests? They'll probably look at our teeth the same way men examine donkeys."

Rebekkah giggled. "Don't even think about that part of it. Just think about being in a royal palace where the furniture is made of ivory and gold and the cushions are covered with blue silk."

"And where all the other girls will chatter and argue and fuss all day long. I'll never have any quiet for reading or doing any of the other things I like," Hadassah retorted.

"But what if the king should choose *you*?" Rebekkah looked at Hadassah with critical eyes. "Goodness knows you're pretty enough."

"Nonsense!" Hadassah's answer was blunt. "I'm no prettier than dozens of girls. The whole thing is stupid. I'm sure the king won't choose me, but if I'm even considered seriously, I'll be forced to stay in his harem the rest of my life."

"You'll be treated almost like royalty," Rebekkah argued. "I understand that the girls in the harem have jewels and silk dresses. There are banquets sometimes, and—" She came to a halt. "What could possibly be wrong with a life like that?"

"Everything!" For a few seconds, Hadassah stalked along in silence. Then she said in a softer voice, "I want to stay with Uncle Mordecai for a few more years. Then, since all Jewish girls have to marry, I'd like to marry some nice ordinary boy someday, like your Joakim. And I want to have children."

"Well, of course. Everyone wants to have children," Rebekkah said.

"But, don't you see? If the king doesn't choose me to be his queen—and of course he won't—I'll just be *nothing*. A silly member of a silly harem eating too much and getting fat and maybe never having children. That's the law, you know."

Rebekkah looked at Hadassah with round eyes. "I never thought of that. Maybe you do have a right to be unhappy."

"Unhappy? I'm miserable! But I'd do anything in the world for Uncle Mordecai, and his mind is made up about this."

"Have you explained how you feel?" Rebekkah asked.

"Of course. But he just looks at me and smiles patiently and says we should leave it in Yahweh's hands."

"Well, if your uncle honestly believes that Yahweh wants you to enter the king's contest—"

Hadassah's next words came out so softly that they were nearly a whisper. "Sometimes I wonder whether Yahweh still cares about us Jews so far away from Jerusalem."

"Don't be silly!" Rebekkah said stoutly. "We're the children of the one true God, and he'll always care about us."

They had reached the well, and they took their places at the end of the line of women and girls waiting to draw water. From where she stood, Hadassah could see the royal placard that announced the king's search for a queen. She knew that similar placards, written in various languages, had been posted throughout the empire of King Ahasuerus. At that very moment, Indian and Ethiopian and Babylonian and Median girls were probably looking at the same announcement. She wondered how many were seeing it with the hollow feeling that she felt.

Hadassah turned to Rebekkah and whispered, "I hope you're right. I hope Yahweh cares about *me.* Otherwise, I don't see how I'm going to stand it."

"When do you go for the first test?"

"Tomorrow."

"So soon?" Rebekkah looked startled.

"The girls of Shushan are to meet in the market square at noon tomorrow."

"Then, when will I see you again?"

"Tomorrow evening, I hope," Hadassah said. "If they reject me, then I'll come directly home."

"But if they don't?"

"Then, I don't know. If I pass every test, I suppose it's possible that we might never see each other again."

Rebekkah didn't answer. She only put out her hand to grip Hadassah's tightly.

"Move up, move up," commanded the girl behind them in the line.

"So you see," Hadassah whispered to Rebekkah as they inched forward, "you better hope that the king's men will think I'm ugly."

While Mordecai was saying his morning prayers the next day, Hadassah put out the food for breakfast, and then quickly kneaded dough for the day's baking and set it out to rise.

Mordecai came into the central room. He glanced at the dough before he looked at Hadassah. "And when do you plan to find time to bake it?" he asked mildly.

"Rebekkah promised to get it and bake it in their oven. I kept some meal from yesterday and only added the leaven this morning. I want fresh bread for your supper."

"My dear," Mordecai began. But then his voice broke and he stopped and looked into her eyes.

Hadassah forced herself to smile. "I've probably worried for nothing. If I'm lucky, the first examiner will shout, 'Take her away,' and I can come home and do my own baking."

"On the contrary," Mordecai said, seating himself on the floor, "by suppertime you'll be established in a fine room with a silk robe and a soft pillow."

"And nothing to read," Hadassah mourned. "Do you suppose you could bring me something to read? If the worst thing possible happens and they accept me, that is."

"Don't be ridiculous. You'll be in the building right next to the palace, not too far from the gate where I'm stationed. I understand the palace has one of the finest libraries in the world. You'll be able to have a hundred scrolls for every one that I've managed to borrow."

Her face brightened. "Honestly? Then, maybe I'll be able to endure it."

Mordecai's face grew sober. "You'll do well to depend on something beside books for your strength. You'll do well to turn to Yahweh, your God, for all your needs."

Hadassah could not meet his eyes. She was remembering all the nights after her parents had been murdered when, in her grief, she had refused to pray to God. It didn't seem likely that Yahweh would listen to her now. But she couldn't say that to Uncle Mordecai.

"I'll try," she said meekly, starting to pick up the bowls that had held milk and olives and pieces of goat cheese. "I'll honestly try."

"And now," Mordecai said, his voice eager, "what are you going to do to make yourself beautiful?"

She stood staring down at him, a bowl balanced in each hand. "I washed my hair yesterday, and my robe and shawl are clean. What else would I do?"

Morecai shook his head. "You were young when your mother died, so you never learned the skills girls use to make themselves lovely. And I'm tco ignorant to teach you."

"Oh, that!" Hadassah's voice was scornful. "Putting kohl on my eyelids, you mean, so that I look as though someone had hit me and bruised my eye?"

"It's to make your eyes look larger."

"They'll have to take me the way I am," Hadassah muttered. "I don't have any kohl, and I don't plan to go out looking for any."

Mordecai shrugged. "I've let you get very stubborn and outspoken," he said with regret. "I hope you'll be more polite when you meet the king's representatives."

"I can only be me."

"And I can only trust Yahweh," Mordecai answered. "Now stack the bowls. I'll wash them later."

"No." Her voice was stubborn. "Let me wash them. Let me leave this house as neat as possible. If I come home later, it will be waiting for me. If I don't, then at least it will be clean for you."

He watched her without comment, and she was grateful for his silence. She didn't want to cry, but she was afraid that if the conversation went on much longer, the tears would start. Then her eyelids would be not only unblackened but also swollen.

If I thought it would make me ugly enough, I'd cry on purpose, she thought. Almost immediately, she put the thought aside as evil. She could never deliberately fail

Mordecai. After all, he had given her a home and hope and love when everything else had been snatched from her by the thieving Amalekites.

She lifted her head abruptly. "Will there be Amalekites among the girls, do you think?"

"Possibly. The kingdom of King Ahasuerus stretches incredibly far. Amalekite girls might strive for the honor of being queen."

"They'd better not come near me." Her chin went up, and her eyes were blazing. "I couldn't be civil to one if I tried."

Mordecai's face was stern. "You can be civil to anyone if necessary. You will not—I've told you this before—you will *not* tell anyone you are a Jew. Not anyone. If you act as though you hate Amalekites, people will wonder. You must treat everyone alike."

"I don't know whether I can or not."

He walked over to her and tilted her face up to his. "You can do anything you have to do. Anything. Yahweh will give you the strength."

His hand was so warm and steady under her chin, his eyes so kind, and his mouth so firm that she felt as though his strength and faith were flowing into her.

"Will you pray for me?" she whispered.

He nodded. "Every day, my daughter. As I have done since the first day you came to my door."

"Then," she said, her voice held steady by force, "then, I expect I'll manage."

She brushed a light kiss on his cheek and hurried into her room. Rubbing a drop of oil into her hands, she smoothed her palms over her hair. Then quickly she formed a long braid which she let hang down her back.

She adjusted her coarse, homespun robe of white cotton and, after a minute of thought, tied a red cord around her waist. She had no sandals other than the leather ones she wore every day, so she gave them only a glance. Picking up the sheer shawl that had been her mother's, she draped it over her head, pulled it across her shoulders, and tucked the ends into the cord at her waist.

For a long moment she remained looking about the small room. She told herself that there was no point in just standing there, but still she stood.

Awkwardly, she clasped her hands and bent her head. "Yahweh, God of Israel," she breathed, "if I matter to you, bless me."

She lifted her head, grateful that she had not started to cry. Without another look at the room, she hurried to where Mordecai stood waiting.

"I'm ready," she announced.

"Then we'll go," Mordecai said.

He started out of the house at his usual rapid pace, the long skirts of his robe flapping around his bare ankles. Hadassah, lifting her shawl so that it partially covered her face, followed him toward the marketplace.

6

Trial in the Silken Tent

The marketplace was jammed with people, and everywhere Hadassah looked, she saw girls. It was an incredible sight. One rarely saw girls out in public except for the daily line at the wells or occasionally at the market stalls. And then they were always dressed in their drabbest clothes, with veils pulled over their faces.

Now the square was awash with color. Girls dressed in crimson and saffron, indigo and ivory, stood with nervous fathers or servants. The attendants were constantly smoothing hair, tugging at a veil, or applying a last-minute touch of kohl. *In public*, Hadassah thought with scorn.

In the very center of the square, a large tent, fashioned of white silk and decorated with purple streamers, had been erected. Hadassah looked all around her, finding some odd comfort in what she was seeing. Every time a servant's nervous fussing pulled a veil momentarily aside, Hadassah could see the face of one of the girls. She was reassured by the heavy use of cosmetics, the artificial curls that hung about the flushed faces. If this was the kind of girl the king wanted, then she was as good as eliminated already.

She tried to catch Mordecai's eye, but he was looking around with such bewilderment that she knew he would not share her feeling of relief. *Well, it's his own fault for thinking I should submit myself to this silly process*, Hadassah thought, trying to harden her heart against him. In spite of all her efforts, she could not suppress a small sense of regret that he was going to be so disappointed when she wasn't chosen.

Each girl, entering the marketplace, had been given a numbered token. As the numbers were called, the girls were ushered into the tent. It soon became obvious to Hadassah that most of the girls were quickly ushered out again through a back door. The wailing and weeping that took place there indicated clearly that these were the girls who had been rejected. Once in a while a girl would be led out a side door, where she seemed to disappear into a group of servants who were milling around.

"When they call me," Hadassah said, "you go around by that back door. See? I'll meet you there, and we can hurry home and get out of this crowd."

Mordecai only smiled.

A minute later, the number on Hadassah's token was called.

"It's me," Hadassah said, and for one second all courage deserted her.

Mordecai leaned toward her and touched his lips to her forehead. "Go, my daughter," he whispered. "Go in the peace of Yahweh."

He raised his hand to attract the attention of the young man who called the numbers, and Hadassah felt herself being pushed gently into the silken tent. Her heart pounded, and her mouth felt dry, but she kept her chin up and did not flinch from the steady stares of the men who stood inside the tent.

"Can you believe it?" one of the men said. "Here's the first one whose face we won't have to wash."

"Had you heard we were washing off the kohl and lip rouge?" another asked. "Did you anticipate that?"

"I never wear kohl," Hadassah said in a voice that came out more sharply than she intended. "I haven't time for such nonsense."

Another man stepped forward. "Well, you'll save us some time. Open your mouth."

Furious, she did as she was told. It was just as humiliating as she had predicted to Rebekkah.

"Her teeth are good. Skin clear. Hair clean and thick. And the color in her cheeks and lips is natural." The announcement was made in a bored voice, and the eyes that examined her face so closely somehow did not see *her* at all.

She longed to make a bitter remark, but her love for Mordecai silenced her. If she were sent from the tent in disgrace, he would be grieved and shamed. She could afford to wait a few more minutes.

An impersonal hand pulled her robe up to her knees and pushed her sleeves up to her shoulders. "Well formed," a voice said.

The first man, the one who had been so astonished at Hadassah's lack of cosmetics, came over to her. Taking her by the arm, he turned her around, studying her intently. "Lovely," he said in the tone of voice a man would use to describe the texture of cloth. "Truly lovely."

Hadassah's breath seemed to stop. She protested, "Not compared to all those other girls."

"What do you know about it?" The man's face crinkled into an unexpected smile. "I am Hegai, head of the king's harem. I know." He turned to the scribe, who had been jotting down the points mentioned in Hadassah's favor. "Send this one to the harem. Send her to section seven." He nodded at Hadassah. "I'm in charge there."

She couldn't answer. It was all she could do to keep from grabbing his arms and begging him to send her home instead.

Hegai's eyes narrowed. "Don't be unhappy," he said kindly. "I'll see that you're properly cared for. You don't have to worry."

Grateful for the fact that Hegai looked at her as a person instead of a thing, Hadassah tried to smile.

"Your name?" the scribe barked.

"Hadassah."

Hegai shook his head. "It will never do. It's not Persian enough. Let's see—what names haven't we used?" But before the scribe could begin to rattle off a list of names, Hegai lifted his hand. "Never mind. We'll call her Esther. It means 'star,' " he added to Hadassah. "It's very suitable. From now on, you'll be called Esther." He turned away from her. "Next," he called.

A young slave touched Hadassah's arm, indicating that she should follow him. She stumbled after him blindly, with only one thought in her mind: She had told Mordecai to wait for her by the door where the rejected girls left the tent. She'd never see him again. Never.

The slave spoke. "Come, my lady. Follow me. We're going to the palace. Have you anything to be carried?"

She shook her head wordlessly. It had never even occurred to her to bring anything with her.

"Don't worry." The voice was Mordecai's, and Hadassah spun toward him with a cry of joy. "I'll bring anything she needs. I'm a gatekeeper at the south gate of the compound wall, and I'm her—a friend of her family."

The slave's face was friendly. "She won't need a thing. And I recognize you, sir. I've seen you at the gate. Everything she'll ever need will be provided. I just thought she might have brought some souvenir."

"I didn't think I'd be staying," Hadassah said.

"But you notice I was waiting at the proper door," Mordecai said. "I had no doubt, Hadassah."

"Her name is Esther, sir," the slave said in a respectful but firm voice. "From now on, she will never be called by her old name again."

Mordecai nodded. "Esther. It's a good name for a Persian girl. So Esther, may you walk in joy."

"And you—" She almost said "my uncle," but caught

herself in time. "May you go in peace." Then formal words deserted her, and she ran to Mordecai in a panic. "Will I see you again? Will I ever see you again?"

"Perhaps. We can't talk," he said slowly, "or not often, at any rate. But if you're in a room that looks south, you'll be able to see me when I go to and from my duties. We can wave, at least."

"I'll see that she gets a south room," the slave said. "Now, come, my lady."

"You see," Mordecai whispered quickly, "already you're a lady. And soon—Yahweh willing—a queen."

She wanted to cry out, "I want only to be your daughter!" Instead she managed to smile as she turned away to follow the young slave out of the marketplace. "I'll look for you," she said. "You can depend on it."

She could hardly see the slave's narrow back for the tears that filled her eyes. Fiercely, she blinked them away and jerked her shawl closer over her face.

The slave turned to look at her. "Are you coming, my lady?"

"Yes," she said clearly. "I'm coming."

The boy grinned. "I've led a half-dozen girls to the palace already today, but you, my lady, make the others look plain. He named you well, Hegai did. I hope I can serve you someday, Lady Esther."

"Why not?" she said lightly, unwilling to reject any gesture of friendship in this strange new life that faced her. "If I'm ever in a position to be served, I'll remember you."

"Thank you. You won't be sorry, my lady. My name is Ator." His smile flashed, and then, in silence, he led the way to the thick wall that surrounded the palace.

7

Ivory and Gold

Everything seems so strange, Esther thought the following day. So many of the familiar little things that had shaped her life were gone: the sound of Mordecai at prayer, the whisper of the breeze in the vines around the door, the soft crackle and hiss of the fire in the small clay oven.

Even the birds are strange, Esther thought sourly as she leaned her arms on the windowsill of the room that had been given to her. A large bird, rattling a fan of iridescent tail feathers, strutted slowly across the yard. Its mate, a drab female, paid no attention to the gorgeous display of purple and bronze feathers.

In spite of her loneliness, Esther found herself giggling a little. The strutting bird was just like the bejeweled and painted girls in the market square, she thought. She wondered if the king would be impressed by all their finery. Or would he be as indifferent as this female bird? She watched the rejected bird finally fold his bright tail feathers and begin to peck disconsolately at the ground, while his mate continued to ignore him.

Esther turned her back to the window and gazed around her room. Instead of a plain mat on the floor, she had a couch for sleeping. It was carved of lovely, dark wood, and had ivory inlaid in an intricate pattern on the legs. Cushions with gold tassels were piled on the cover of scarlet silk.

A sound at her door caught her attention, and she looked up to see Hegai, the man who had talked to her in the silken tent the day before, standing in the opening.

"Good morning," he said. "I saw you watching the birds outside your window a moment ago. They were brought here from Egypt. They're called peacocks. Aren't they beautiful?"

"Yes, they are," Esther said tonelessly.

Hegai's voice took on a note of concern. "Are you well?"

She nodded. "I'm well."

"You're still wearing your own robe," he said. "Why haven't you put on the clothes that were laid out for you?"

She glanced at the shimmering robe of ivory silk that lay across the couch. "I thought it was to be saved for some special event. Such as when I go to see the king."

Hegai laughed. "That's only one of the many robes

that will be yours to wear. Your own is only fit to be thrown away."

Her chin went up. "I'd feel silly sitting around in silk all day. What do girls *do* around here?"

Hegai laughed again. His face was soft and plump, and his hands were as white as a woman's. Esther knew about men like Hegai, men who were called eunuchs. They were good for only one thing—to guard the women in harems or in palaces. *At least*, Esther thought with gratitude, *he looks kind.*

Hegai was answering her question. "They learn how to be beautiful," he said. "And they learn how to walk and talk and dress so that they might delight the king."

Esther felt a great desire to say that it all sounded boring, but Uncle Mordecai had always insisted on good manners.

"I don't suppose," she said instead, "I don't suppose it would be possible for me to have something to read?"

Hegai looked at her in astonishment. "Read? A girl read?"

He looked so amazed that Esther could not help smiling. "My—the man who escorted me to the market square is more of a scholar than a gatekeeper," she confided. "He works as a gatekeeper to earn enough money to eat. But he reads in every spare minute. Because he had no sons, and because he loves to teach, he taught me. I have grown to love to read."

"It might make you squint," Hegai said doubtfully.

She laughed aloud. "In this bright room? The room at home was much darker than this."

"I'll look into it," Hegai said after a pause. "I can't promise anything, of course."

"Of course not. But if you find something—"

"What do you prefer?"

"I never had any choice. I just read whatever came to my hands." She remembered the scrolls that told of the lives of Yahweh's people, stories of Abraham and Isaac and Moses. How indifferent she had been when Uncle Mordecai had brought them home, taking them for granted. Now she'd dearly love to have them. "Stories of history and gods and things like that," she added. "I'd love those."

"More than accounts of purchases and scales?" Hegai's eyes were twinkling.

"I've even read those," she admitted. A sudden thought struck her. "I know. If there are scrolls that tell of King Ahasuerus, of his deeds and of his family, I'd like those."

"Well, I'll try," Hegai said again. He started to turn away and then looked back at her. "By the way, I came to tell you that seven servants will be sent to you. Maidens to dress and undress you. Slaves to bathe you and train you in the arts of perfume. Girls to teach you how to talk and act."

She stared at him in astonishment. "If they're slaves, how do they know all these things?"

"Some of them were princesses," Hegai said. "When King Ahasuerus goes into battle, all captives become slaves. And he doesn't capture only the peasants, you know."

Esther shook her head. "I can't believe a common girl like me could have princesses for slaves."

Hegai smiled again. "You're a refreshing change from the spoiled, selfish girls who fill most of these rooms. You can be sure I'll find the finest slaves available for you. And," he tossed over his shoulder, "if there are any scrolls available—"

"I've heard that the royal palace has one of the best libraries in the world," Esther could not help saying.

Hegai grinned. "You know that, do you? Then I guess I'll have to find something."

After he left, Esther sat on the foot of the couch, staring out her window. Her patience was rewarded in a little while when she saw Mordecai walk toward the south gate. He kept his eyes decorously away from the harem wall. Just as he was opposite her window, she whistled a few soft notes.

He looked up then, and their eyes met. She forced her lips to smile. It was bad enough, she thought, that *she* was miserable. There was no use making him miserable, too. The least she could do every day was smile. His expression of pride and delight was something she could hold in her heart all day to help her endure the lonely hours.

"May I bring your breakfast, my lady?" The soft voice spoke heavily accented but correct Persian.

Esther looked away from the window to see a girl with skin the color of old ivory, the beauty of her face ruined by a puckered scar on her cheek. The branding of slaves had always seemed cruel to Esther, yet she supposed there was no other way to keep a daring slave from trying to run away.

"Breakfast? Yes, of course," Esther said, feeling a little foolish. How, exactly, did one speak to a slave?

"My name is Suhas, my lady. My lord, Hegai, has chosen me to be your personal slave."

For a few seconds, Esther was uncertain what to do or say next. Then her common sense asserted itself. There was no use trying to pretend to be something she wasn't. The girl would find out soon enough.

"I've never been served by a slave before," Esther admitted with a smile. "I may do everything wrong."

Suhas's eyes widened in astonishment. "And I, my lady," she confided as she set her metal tray on a low table, "I had slaves waiting on me every day of my life until I was captured by the Persian soldiers."

They stood staring at each other. "Then you'll have to teach me," Esther said. "It's not our fault that I have to be served or that you have to do the serving. We're both here because of the way things are. So we'll just have to make the best of it."

Suhas looked at Esther for a long minute before her eyes dropped humbly. "Yes, my lady," she said, "I'll do all I can for you."

"So," Esther said practically, "where do I sit and what do I do?"

She was rewarded with a smile from Suhas that Esther hoped would soon blossom into loyalty and friendship.

Esther had been in the palace three days when Hegai appeared again at her door, with Ator trailing behind him. The slave boy's arms were filled with piles of scrolls, some of them dusty with age, a few clean and new, some tied with frayed cord, others tied with bright strips of cloth. At Hegai's command, the boy dumped the scrolls onto Esther's couch.

"There," Hegai said. "Does that please you?"

Esther clasped her hands to prevent herself from actually clapping. "Marvelous!" she cried. "I've never seen so many scrolls together at one time. It's like having a treasure of riches."

Hegai's eyes skimmed over the elaborate furnishings of the room and touched lightly on the gold bracelets that circled Esther's wrists and ankles. "There are many kinds of riches," he said dryly.

She felt her cheeks grow warm with embarrassment. "I'm aware of how many lovely things there are in this room," she said stiffly. "But riches for the mind, that's the most exciting thing of all."

Hegai changed the subject. "The man who brought you to the market square—I see him every day going by the palace."

"He's the man who taught me to read," she said. "He's a gatekeeper for the king, and he goes by my window on his way to and from his place of work. I always wave at him. Is that wrong?"

Hegai spoke slowly. "If you had demanded the right to wave at him, it might have been forbidden. Because you're never greedy or demanding, I'm willing to grant you the right to even speak to him occasionally."

"Oh, thank you—" Esther fumbled to a stop, not sure what title to give the man who looked at her almost as a father would.

"Just call me Hegai," he said. "The other girls call me by my title. I want you to call me by my name."

"Thank you. And thank you for the scrolls. You've been kinder than I had ever dreamed anyone would be."

Hegai glanced across the room to Suhas, who was standing quietly by the window. "Does the lady Esther accept the instruction of the seven girls I sent to train and serve her?"

Suhas nodded. "She moves slowly in the field of cosmetics, my lord. But rapidly in the field of the graces."

"I must admit," Hegai said lightly, "that it's a relief to come into her room. Some of the others are so cloyed with perfume I think I've walked inside a scent bottle."

Esther was so busy pulling the string off the newest-looking scroll that she paid little attention to the conversation.

"The drapes are never pulled across the window here," Suhas said. "Lady Esther likes fresh air. She isn't interested in using a lot of perfume and cosmetics, my lord."

"Let her go her own way. If she's a refreshing change for me, who knows? She might also be a refreshing change for the king."

Esther looked up from the scroll she was holding. "This tells of the achievements of King Ahasuerus," she said. "They seem almost unending: his crushing of the revolt in Egypt, his assembling the largest army in the world to battle Greece. If he has done so many wonderful things, why does he look so unhappy?"

Hegai looked astonished. "How could you know what he looks like? Common people never see his face."

"It was an accident," Esther confessed. "One day his carriage passed me on the street, and the wind blew the curtain aside. I've never told anyone about it before, because I know I wasn't supposed to see him. But he was so . . . bored looking that I've never been able to forget."

"One does not speak of the king in such a way." Hegai's voice was very stern. "One speaks of the king only in terms of praise."

Esther glanced down at the scroll in her hands and then looked up again. "I guess I should have known that. I'd just been hoping that the king would find happiness. That's all."

Hegai's eyes met Suhas's, and they exchanged a strange look.

"Take very good care of her," Hegai said softly. "Compassion is as rare in young women as modesty."

"I know, my lord," Suhas said in her light, pretty voice. "In my country of India, she would be truly appreciated."

"And well she might be here," Hegai murmured.

Esther, her head bent over the scroll, hardly heard their words. She was caught up in the deeds of the majestic and mighty king of the great Persian empire. But even in the midst of the flowery, flattering phrases, she was remembering the sullen look of the young king in his chariot. She wondered if anyone, even his historians, cared how he really felt.

8

Next in Line

Slowly, many months went by. Comforted by her reading and her growing affection for Suhas, Esther managed to endure the days. Hegai always seemed to know when her homesickness was worst, and would arrange things so that Mordecai could stand outside the window and speak to her. True, they could say nothing private or important, but at least they could exchange ideas. They could discuss the marvelous tales of history and mythology Esther was reading, and best of all, she could see the love in his eyes.

Other girls were called, one by one, into the king's presence. Sometimes Esther walked by the rooms as the great flutter of preparation was going on. She would gaze in astonishment at the anointing and curling and dressing that took place.

"You know," Esther confided to Suhas one evening, "I'm beginning to believe that my name will never be drawn. I'll spend the rest of my life listening to the squeals of girls when they are invited to visit the king, and their wailing when they aren't chosen to be queen."

Suhas giggled a little. "You'll be called, my lady. There aren't many girls left, so surely your name will be drawn soon."

"When it is," Esther announced in a warning tone, "don't think for one minute that I'm going to make the silly fuss that these other girls have made. I'm not going to drown myself in perfume or torture myself winding my hair in curls.

"But it would be nice if I could have new sandals," she added as an afterthought. "I love those fine leather sandals with straps that wrap around your ankles. Do you suppose I could have some of those?"

"You don't seem to understand, my lady. You can have anything you want."

"Anything except my freedom," Esther retorted.

It wasn't many more weeks before Hegai was standing in the doorway, his face flushed with excitement. "Well, Esther, my child," he said quickly, "the time has come. Your name has just been pulled in the lottery."

Esther's mouth went dry. "*My* name?"

"Yes. Tomorrow evening, just before dinner is served, you'll be taken to the king's apartment."

"Perhaps he won't raise his scepter toward me," Esther suggested with a nervous little giggle. "Then I'll be sentenced to death even before I have a chance to speak to him."

Hegai frowned. "Don't talk foolishly."

"But it's true," Esther insisted. "I've heard it many times. If the king doesn't point his scepter toward the person coming into his chamber, the person dies."

"Well, of course." Hegai's voice was impatient. "But you've been invited. The king accepts the presence of anyone who has been especially invited."

"I guess I knew that," Esther admitted. "It's just that, well, I don't think I ever believed this day would come."

"She doesn't want to wear the customary cosmetics, sir," Suhas said. "And she doesn't plan to curl her hair. I don't know—"

"Let her do what she wants," Hegai said, interrupting. "It's obvious that all the bejeweled, ornate girls who have been taken to the king so far haven't pleased him." He turned to Esther. "I have great hopes for you, little one. I believe you have the intelligence and compassion and courage to be a queen. Don't fail me."

Esther stared at the man who had done so much to make these many months bearable for her. He, like Mordecai, counted on her to please the king.

"I'll try," Esther whispered meekly. A sudden thought came to her. "If the king doesn't like me, I'll be sent over to the other harem after tomorrow. Will I ever see you again?"

"Let's think only that the king *will* like you," Hegai said. "Then I'll see you every day. Once the queen has been chosen, I'll be assigned to her apartment. Hathach and I will be the queen's personal servants."

Esther tried to smile. "That's a real reason for making me want to please the king."

Hegai looked at her fondly. "If I believed in gods," he said softly, "I'd pray that the king's heart would be warmed toward you."

Several hours later, Ator tapped on Esther's door. "My lady," he said eagerly, "I saw your friend, the keeper of the south gate, and told him you were to go to the king. I asked Hegai if he might speak to you."

Esther smiled affectionately at the boy. "How good of you," she said.

Leaning from her window a short time later, Esther gazed down into the face of Mordecai. She tried to keep her voice light. "The time has come for me to visit the king."

"I'm grateful," Mordecai said. "Another month or two, and I might have started to get really nervous."

She laughed. "I'm nervous now," she confided.

Mordecai looked over his shoulder at Ator, who had brought him to Esther's window and now squatted on the ground behind him. Like any well-trained servant, the boy was making no attempt to listen.

"You don't have to be nervous," Mordecai insisted. "Not if you follow all the things I taught you."

She was sure he was trying to tell her she could turn to Yahweh for help. "I know," she nodded. "But I'm not very good at—lots of things. Sometimes I think that the only thing I really do well is read."

"But you read for a purpose," Mordecai argued. "You learn about great kings and queens and warriors. And about simple women, women like Sarah and Hannah and Rachel."

They were ordinary names, Esther realized. Names that might belong to many girls in the city of Shushan. But they were also the names of women who had prayed to Yahweh. They had asked for impossible things, but their God had granted their requests.

"Just ordinary women," Esther murmured.

"No one," Mordecai said sternly, "is truly ordinary. Each person in the world has a special value. When you enter the king's presence tomorrow, go with the knowledge that you may have been chosen."

"I won't know what to do or say," Esther said in a soft voice of despair.

"Just tell yourself that the king is a man," Mordecai advised. "He wears a royal crown of gold, and he has power beyond belief, but sometimes he is lonely or cold or tired. Think of that. It may help."

"I'll try," Esther promised.

"I'll pray for you." That much Mordecai dared say without revealing that he was a Jew, Esther realized. After all, all men, Jews or Persians or Ethiopians, had gods to whom they prayed.

"I'll pray, too," Esther said. "I may not know the proper words, but I'll pray."

"Then I won't be nervous any longer." Mordecai drew in a long breath. "If praying could become your habit, then everything would be all right."

Esther knew he must long to quote some words from the holy Scripture, some psalm of the great King David or some promise of one of the prophets.

"If the king doesn't favor me, I'll be in the permanent harem after tomorrow," Esther said. "I've heard that a man named Shaashgaz is in charge there. Perhaps you can persuade him to be as generous as Hegai has been, and perhaps we can still talk sometimes."

Mordecai smiled. "I doubt very much that I'll ever have to cultivate Shaashgaz's friendship. After all, the queen of Persia has an apartment of her own, and her own servants. She doesn't stay in the harem."

"Well," Esther said, smiling at his faith, "we'll just wait and see. Whatever happens, don't ever forget that—I love you."

He lifted his hand and his lips moved. She knew he was praying for her and she bowed her head in the way she had been taught.

"At least you'll let me scent the bathwater with rose petals, won't you, my lady?" Suhas's voice was pleading.

"Do they do that in India?" Esther asked with curiosity. She had slept poorly the night before, and her heart kept jumping into her throat in spite of her determination to be calm.

"Yes. And other fragrant herbs. If you'll let me scent the water—only lightly, I promise, my lady—then at least there will be a drift of fragrance about you."

"When I was little," Esther said, "my mother used to twist wild flowers in my hair. I suppose it would be nearly the same. I'd like to do something my mother would have liked."

"And your robe?"

Esther was silent a moment. "Something very plain and simple," she said. "I'm not being silly about this. I'm really just a girl who loves to knead bread, who enjoys the feel of weaving thread into sturdy cloth. The king should see me as I really am, not as some fancy doll."

Suhas nodded her head. "You're right, my lady, and wise to recognize it. Don't worry. I'll fix you so you'll be satisfied, and if we're lucky, the king will be, too."

Several hours later, Esther stood in the center of her room while Suhas stepped back to examine her.

"You look just the way you want to, my lady," she said with satisfaction. "You look lovely. Now if you'll only smile as you do with me, and say funny things occasionally as you do with Hegai, and move gracefully, as Lora taught you to, everything will be fine."

"I'll do my best," Esther said, her voice catching.

"You're ready, my lady?" Hegai stood at the door. He was flanked by two slave boys, each bearing a torch. One of them, Esther saw, was Ator.

She smiled at the man and at the boys. "I'm ready. I may not be able to say a single word, but I'm ready."

The boys grinned at her frankness. They bowed and backed away from the door to make room for her to come out. She hesitated and then turned back to Suhas.

"Wait for me," Esther whispered.

"Forever, my lady." Suhas's eyes held the love that Esther had hoped for.

"And you won't forget my scrolls?" Esther begged, turning to Hegai.

"No, my child. You'll have everything you need."

Esther drew a deep breath and straightened her shoulders. Then she said in a clear, steady voice, "Will you lead me to my lord, King Ahasuerus?"

9

Ahasuerus

Hegai swung open the door that led to the king's chamber and announced in a loud voice, "The lady Esther of Shushan, to see the king!"

Esther, her heart pounding, stood in the doorway, blinking in the light of what seemed like a thousand torches. Slowly she walked across the wide room to where the golden throne rested on its dais. At first, because the light flickered and moved, and because her eyes were dazzled, she could not see the king's face. She could see only the glitter of the crown on his head and the rich sheen of the purple robe that swept to the floor. In spite of Hegai's reassurance, her eyes went immediately to the scepter in the king's hand. As she saw it lift toward her, she drew a deep breath of relief.

The breath seemed to steady her heart and make it possible for her to walk closer to the throne. Remembering Lora's instructions, she moved lightly across the dark, polished floor and knelt in front of the most powerful monarch in the world, waiting silently for him to speak.

"Esther," Ahasuerus said in a drawl. "What particular heavens do you belong in?"

She had expected coldness, or indifference, or even a show of admiration. She had not expected humor. She felt a bubble of laughter take the place of the fear that had filled her.

"Whatever heavens my lord allows me to inhabit," she said, letting her eyes come up to meet his. "I only hope that it will be a very small heaven—so I won't shine too dimly."

He laughed aloud. "At least you didn't pretend not to know what I was talking about," he observed with satisfaction. "Here, come and sit beside me." He stood up and put out his hand to lift her to her feet.

Taking his hand, she moved with him to sit in the chair he indicated. The chair, of smooth, polished wood inlaid with flowers and vines made of pearl and coral, was cushioned with scarlet.

The king looked critically at her. "Didn't anyone offer you jewels, or more elaborate clothes?" he asked abruptly.

"Oh, yes, my lord," she answered. "It was my choice to wear only these bracelets that had been my mother's. As for the dress, well, I'm a plain girl. I didn't want to deceive my lord."

"Do you think I'd be easy to deceive?" His voice held a mixture of amusement and peevishness.

She met his eyes squarely. Could she risk honesty? "All men are surely deceived a little, my lord," she murmured, smiling. "They'd be amazed if they could see what girls go through to make themselves appear to be what they aren't."

She held her breath, but released it when his eyes began to twinkle.

"You mean," he said with pretended astonishment, "that their eyelashes aren't really that black? That they weren't born reeking of perfume? That their lips aren't actually as red as they seem?"

She had to swallow the giggle that crowded into her throat. "Perhaps my lord sees more than the average man. I'm glad I didn't try to fool him."

"You have my permission to address me as 'you' rather than 'him,' " Ahasuerus said with a gracious slant of his head, and Esther saw the widening of the eyes of the slaves nearest the throne. Evidently the king did not grant such freedom to everyone.

"Thank you, my lord." Her voice was modest, but she faced the king as squarely as she had always faced Mordecai.

"You're a refreshing change," Ahasuerus admitted. "I've been bored to death with the painted dolls who have been parading across my life for months. And not a thought in their heads except what they've been taught about how to sit or stand or even laugh."

Her answer probably should have been, "Yes, my lord," but instead, she blurted out impulsively, "I knew you were bored, my lord. Even before you began to search for a queen." As she realized what she had said, she grew cold with fear.

Ahasuerus looked at her with sudden awareness, as though at that moment she stopped being something he had to inspect and became a person with an idea that interested him. "What do you mean? Are you saying that you, an ordinary girl in Shushan, dared to judge the king?"

She had brought up the forbidden topic, and now she had to explain. "Not judge, my lord. I saw you one day in your carriage, and I felt sad that you were alone and . . . unhappy."

He sat staring at her, and a variety of emotions flashed across his face. She was sure she saw momentary anger, but curiosity took its place.

"You mean," Ahasuerus said slowly, "that you thought of me as a man, just a man who might be *lonely?*"

"Yes, my lord," she said recklessly. "I wanted the king to find happiness."

"And what does a king need in order to be happy?" he inquired coldly.

"I would think," she began, choosing her words carefully, "that everyone in the world needs to be loved for himself. Even the gods and goddesses of mythology have a consort to love."

"What could you know about mythology?" His voice was no longer cold.

She relaxed and risked a smile. "I've been reading a great deal during the months I've been in your palace, my lord. Your library has some wonderful scrolls."

"You read?" His voice sounded astonished.

"Yes, my lord. It's my greatest joy."

He leaned back, crossed his arms, and grinned at her. "Well, if you wanted happiness to come into my life, why didn't you persuade them to draw your name months ago?"

For a long time, she stared at him, not quite sure if his words meant what she thought they did. Finally she said, "I, my lord?"

He leaned forward to tilt her chin up with his fingers. For many seconds, he gazed at her, turning her face first one way and then the other. With his other hand, he touched her hair and smoothed her cheek. At last, he let his hands drop and sat back in his throne.

"You are the loveliest thing I've ever seen," he said. "What's more, you have a mind. If I am as pleased at the end of the evening as I am now, it may be that my search is over."

A thousand answers swirled in and out of her mind. It was completely incredible to her that Ahasuerus had said what he had. Was it possible that she could be a queen?

No, of course not. She almost opened her lips to say so, but something stopped her.

She had come into the king's presence because Mordecai had wanted it, had believed Yahweh could make her queen. Not for one minute had she thought that she would have any desire to be queen. Now, to her complete astonishment, she discovered that she felt drawn to the man in the golden throne as she had never been drawn to anyone else except Mordecai.

She looked into the king's eyes. "I will try to please you, my lord," she said breathlessly.

Ahasuerus smiled at her and clapped his hands. "Come," he said to the slave beside him. "Let the evening's entertainment begin. Bring the dancers and the jugglers. Serve food to Esther and me. Have musicians come."

Esther, accustomed to the simplicity of Mordecai's house and to the solitude of the room in which she had spent well over a year, stared in astonishment. Cymbals and harps and drums created music so loud that it hurt her ears. Dancing girls, with costumes so scanty that Esther felt her cheeks burning, twisted into amazing acrobatic positions. And jugglers tossed colored balls into the air with an agility that delighted her.

Several times she turned to glance at the king, and each time she found his eyes on her. She could not hope to hide from him the fact that she winced when the music got too loud, or looked at the floor in embarrassment when the dancing girls first appeared, or laughed with delight at the deftly tossed balls. It would be difficult, she realized, to hide any of her feelings from this man.

The noise swirled around them while the elaborately prepared foods appeared like magic on a table drawn up in front of the two chairs. Esther's head was throbbing.

Abruptly, Ahasuerus waved his hands. "Enough," he said. "The lady tires of the noise."

"How did you know, my lord?"

"Your face gives you away. I think the only thing you really liked was the jugglers."

"They're so clever," she said. "I can't believe that their hands are quick enough to catch the balls."

"It's all a matter of practice," Ahasuerus claimed. He stood and put out his hand. One of the jugglers, bowing low, came up to the king and placed three bright balls in his palm.

Ahasuerus looked at Esther with the mischievous glance of a boy. "See!" he said proudly as the balls ascended and descended, flowing through his hands and over his head.

Without thinking, Esther clapped her hands with delight. "You're as clever as any of the jugglers, my lord. I wish I could learn."

"Why not? Here, come and try."

At first, no matter how often she tried to imitate the king's agile hands, she always dropped one of the balls. Each time, one of the slaves scrambled after it and put it back into her hands.

"I'm so clumsy!"

"No, here. It's a matter of rhythm. Lift your hands, one at a time, and keep your eyes on the balls."

This time she managed to toss the balls several times before one tumbled to the floor.

"You're a marvelous teacher, my lord," she said, laughing with pleasure. "It had never occurred to me to watch the balls. I was looking at my hands."

Ahasuerus grinned. "You can practice all you want after you become queen."

Her hands became very still. She stood clutching the little balls, staring up at the young man with the dark curls who was so much taller than she.

"You're the first to make me laugh and to make me curious about what goes on in your mind," he said. "I've made my decision."

"I hope you won't regret it, my lord." Her voice was very subdued.

Ignoring the slaves who stood in the room and the entertainers who were leaving, Ahasuerus came over to Esther. Taking the balls out of her hands, he put his arms around her. She felt herself tremble.

"You're very young," he said against her cheek, too quietly for anyone else to hear. "Do you think, even so, you can learn to love me?"

She had never known that such a strange blend of joy and shyness could fill her. The feeling reminded her of the song Solomon had written. She raised her eyes to the king's.

"I think, my lord," she said very softly, very honestly, "that I will learn to love you sooner than I would have believed possible. I pray that you will also . . . love me."

"Love you?" His voice was soft also, but his astonishment was obvious to Esther. She had meant the kind of love any ordinary husband and wife in Shushan might have, the kind her parents had had, not the kind a king might have for a woman in a harem made up of many women. And he must have known what she meant.

"It's up to you," he said briefly. "I think if anyone could capture my heart, it might be you."

"Thank you, my lord," she whispered, and realized she would have to be content with that.

Ahasuerus bent his head and kissed her gently. "Now," he announced, "we'll have a great celebration. We'll have a banquet for everyone who is anyone at all. And you, my little one, will sit at my right hand and accept the loyalty of the provinces."

Her heart was still racing from his kiss. *I wonder*, she thought, *if Uncle Mordecai's prayers had asked for this: that I would find happiness, instead of dread, at the thought of becoming queen of Persia.*

10

It's Not Customary, You Know

The following weeks were crowded with preparations for the banquet the king had proposed. The wedding itself had been a simple, businesslike affair on the day after Esther had first visited the king. But the banquet was to be a splendid event. Although Esther herself was not responsible for any of the preparation, a dozen times a day slaves sought audience with her, seeking her opinion on what should be done.

"If we drape the walls with rose silk," one slave asked, "will it go with what you plan to wear, my lady?"

"Do you want dancers first or wrestlers, my lady?" asked another.

"Would you like roast peacock, my lady?" queried a

third. "The cook could serve it so that it looks alive, with the feathers inserted back in the skin."

At first Esther was reluctant to make decisions on these subjects, but the last question brought an emphatic response. "No, no roast peacock," she said, remembering the gorgeous bird in the palace yard who had tried to woo his drab lady. "They're far too lovely to kill."

The young slave scampered off to tell his master of the new queen's opinion, and Esther turned with a sigh of relief to Suhas.

"I almost wish there weren't going to be any banquet," Esther said. "I wish—"

"What, my lady?"

Esther shook her head sadly. "No," she admitted. "No. My wishes are too ridiculous."

She turned to the window and gazed wistfully toward the distant walls that enclosed the king's residence. Now that she was in the queen's apartment, her window faced the eastern end of the palace. She could look out on the high walls that sheltered the king from the world.

Even from me, Esther thought. This was the source of her sadness. She knew she was being foolish, but wouldn't it be nice if instead of king of Persia, Ahasuerus were just a merchant or a farmer or a gatekeeper? Then he would come home at the end of each day, and they could be alone.

She thought back to her childhood, to the way her father had looked at her mother when he came home from his little shop in Babylon, and the way they had talked. Sometimes seriously, sometimes with laughter, but, except for their children, alone.

I've never been alone with the king, Esther thought, *except for the nights I've spent in his sleeping quarters.*

She remembered with pleasure the feel of Ahasuerus's arms around her and of his lips on hers. But surely there was more to marriage than that.

It's not fair, Esther thought as she turned back from the window.

"You can't tell me what it is you wish, my lady?" Suhas persisted.

Esther smiled, pushing her sorrow away. "I was wishing that Ahasuerus were a simple merchant who could spend his evenings with me instead of with his emir and his ministers."

A voice spoke from the open door, and Esther looked up in astonishment and fear to see Ahasuerus standing in the opening.

"Perhaps you wish for another husband," he snapped.

"Oh, no, my lord!" Ignoring Suhas and the servant who stood behind the king, she hurried to Ahasuerus. "I would rather see you rarely than any other man frequently."

"You say that only out of courtesy," he complained. Then, before she could answer, he snapped out orders. "Leave us, you two. Take all the servants and attendants from the queen's apartment. Leave us alone."

Instead of happiness, Esther felt apprehension. Why was the king doing this? He had never come to her apartment during the day. Had she done something wrong?

"I'm bored," Ahasuerus said, sitting down on a

couch. "I'm tired of granting favors and meting out punishments. I'm sick of complaints and flattery."

She looked at the sulky curve of his mouth, and wondered if he had charged into Vashti's rooms like this. If he had, what had she done?

It doesn't make any difference what Vashti did, Esther's common sense told her. *I'm the queen now. And my husband needs to be challenged, or amused.*

"Would you give me another juggling lesson, my lord?" she suggested, her voice light. "I've been practicing, you know."

A little of the frustration left his face. "Have you really? Let me see how well you do."

She ran to the drawer where she kept the three scarlet balls. Turning to the king, she tried to forget that he was a powerful monarch, and made herself think of him as a man tired of responsibility.

"Watch," she boasted. "I can toss them a dozen times before I drop one."

He watched, smiling, while she tossed and caught the little balls. When one finally fell from her hands to end the show, he applauded lightly.

"Very good," he said. "You must have spent a great deal of time in practice." He patted the cushion beside him, and she sank, flushed and proud, onto the couch.

"There isn't much else to do," she admitted.

He lifted an eyebrow. "Does no one seek your advice about the banquet?"

"Oh, they all come to me," she agreed. "But they have such small details for me to decide."

"I know." He nodded. "A king's life is full of such unimportant decisions. After all, I can't make edicts or conquer the Egyptians or lose to the Greeks every day." He winced, as if the memory of the defeat of his fleet at Salamis still hurt him. "Some of the small details I enjoy—such as the ones about the palace I'm having built at Persepolis. Others I hate. I leave some decisions to my ministers, but then I wonder if they're deceiving me, using me."

"You, my lord? But you're the most powerful man in the whole world."

"Sometimes I feel as though I'm nothing but a puppet being pulled by strings."

She stared at him, astonished. There was no question about his sincerity, but she found it hard to believe that he would make such an admission to her.

"I understand, my lord. I suppose all of us are controlled by others at times. Through force, or clever persuasion. Or sometimes because we don't care about a matter."

The last phrase came out with hesitation, and Ahasuerus shot a quick look at her.

"You think I'm indifferent to my duties?" he asked coldly.

"Oh, no, my lord! But surely no one could persuade you to do anything against your will."

"Yes, they can," he admitted abruptly. "I'm not always as forceful as I should be, or as careful."

She considered this, her head tilted to one side. "I think you're forceful when you need to be."

He smiled and leaned back, lacing his fingers behind his head. "I haven't the least idea why I'm saying all this to you. If you repeat any of it, I'll say you're lying."

"Of course, my lord. What you're saying to me is a

private conversation between a man—I beg your pardon, my lord—a *king* and his wife."

Ahasuerus's smile broadened. "You know, you make me feel as domestic as any husband in Shushan," he observed.

She looked at his grin, his relaxed posture, and she felt her throat swell with a great tenderness. "I can't domesticate you any more than I could tame a wolf, my lord. But if you learn to be comfortable around me, I'll be satisfied."

He stared at her. "That's exactly how I feel," he announced in a tone of discovery. "Comfortable. Now, talk to me. Tell me how it came about that you learned to read, you who are merely a girl."

His eyes were teasing, and she smiled at him. But deep inside she felt a twinge of hurt. Could she really be satisfied with the fact that he only felt "comfortable" with her? If she were wholly honest, she would admit she wanted more than that. She wanted him to need and love her as much as she . . .

There! She had admitted it to herself at last. She had grown to love the king. She recalled the words of King Solomon on Mordecai's scroll: "If one were to give all the wealth of his house for love, it would be utterly scorned." It was true. Ahasuerus could not have bought her love. It had come of its own accord. But would he—could he—ever feel that way for her?

She hurried to answer his question, trying to speak lightly. "Well, I was brought up by a family friend, you know, and he . . ." She told what she felt it was safe to tell, making the whole tale sparkle with humor.

Ahasuerus threw back his head and laughed when

she finished. "You probably bewitched the poor old man," he said, "so that he had no choice but to teach you. Just as you've bewitched me."

"Have I, my lord?" she asked and could not keep the wistfulness out of her voice.

"Why else would I leave my duties in the middle of the day, with half of my servants running around in a panic not knowing what to do? Why else would I come to your apartment just to talk?"

"Perhaps just because I wanted you to come so much," she said honestly.

He stared at her for a minute. "Then I'll come again," he said. "It's not customary, you know, but I'll come again."

He kissed her swiftly and turned to leave. "And don't stop practicing," he said with mock severity. "If you become good enough, I'll hire you out as a juggler, and we can make our fortune."

They laughed together. Faint but clear in her memory, Esther could hear the sound of her parents' laughter, like an echo.

11

Rose for a Queen

As the day of the banquet approached, Esther found herself getting more and more nervous.

"I wish it were all over," she said to Suhas. "I wish this were the next day, and all these powerful and important guests were on their way home."

Suhas was shocked. "But, my lady, it will be wonderful. You'll be the most important person there, and everyone will pay you homage."

"What if I do something wrong?" Esther wailed. "What if I embarrass the king or accidentally insult someone?"

Suhas looked stern. "You're not the same girl you were when you came to the palace. You've been taught how to walk and sit and talk. Why would you do anything foolish?"

"I might forget," Esther muttered. "Underneath, where it doesn't show, I still prefer reading and spinning to huge banquets."

"Would you want the king to hear you say that, my lady?"

Esther felt her face growing hot. "Oh, no," she cried. "I would never want him to know I feel like this."

"He commanded that a banquet be held in your honor, my lady," Suhas reminded her. "It would never occur to him that you would find it a burden."

"You shame me," Esther said at last. "I had not thought of his feelings."

"It's not my place to shame you, my lady. But it is my place to encourage and help you."

"I know." Esther smiled at her slave. "You remind me of my—" She stopped. The words *my Uncle Mordecai* had almost tumbled out. Hiding her relationship to him did not get easier. "Of my father," she finished. (Wasn't Mordecai like a father to her?) "He would have said the same thing."

"Then don't worry any more, my lady. Come with me to see the banquet hall. Hegai said we could walk down there this afternoon."

Esther draped a filmy scarf over her face and around her shoulders. She had learned that a queen must hold herself aloof at all times, separating herself from the masses even if only with a veil of sheer cloth. She followed Suhas down the long corridor that led to the banqueting room, looking neither left nor right.

"Look, my lady," Suhas said when they reached the

large arched doorway of the banquet hall.

Esther looked up, and her concern for herself fled instantly. The walls of the great room were draped with rose-colored linen, and the marble pillars were circled with white and scarlet streamers. The tables glittered with golden cups and plates, and the rich scent of roses filled the air. At the head table, which was separated from the rest of the room by a transparent curtain, two golden thrones, cushioned with royal purple, had been placed side by side.

Esther gasped. "I had no idea they could make it look like this. It's gorgeous!"

"Slaves will line the walls, each of them holding a torch," Suhas explained, "so that even if the festivities last until after dark, the room will still be brilliant."

"It's the most beautiful room I've ever seen," Esther announced. But after they had looked their fill and started back down the corridor, she said, "I wish we hadn't gone to see it."

"Why not?"

"Because I wish the king had seen my first reaction. I wish he could know how pleased I am."

"You could pretend you hadn't seen it."

"You know how Persians feel about the importance of telling the truth," Esther protested.

"I don't mean lying, my lady. Most women pretend sometimes. They pretend to be happy when they're sad, rested when they're tired, amused when they're bored. Maybe they think of it as a way of showing love."

Esther was silent, but Suhas's words kept sliding through her mind. She had never thought of that before.

Esther had not been called to the king's rooms for three days, so the day of the banquet was filled with a strange mixture of apprehension and excitement. She was still frightened at the idea of facing hundreds of strangers, but at the same time she could hardly wait to see Ahasuerus again. He had sent word that his preoccupation with the banquet and his duties to visiting dignitaries had made it impossible for him to send for her. But she always worried when she didn't see him.

Suhas started with her grooming preparations early in the day, and Esther patiently endured the bathing, the braiding, the anointing. By late afternoon, she was ready. Her robe of pale pink, girdled with gold, matched the silk bands that had been braided into her dark hair. Shimmering gold and luminous pearls glowed softly in her ears, at her throat, and around her wrists and ankles.

"You're perfect," Suhas said and led the way to the chamber where Hegai was waiting.

"Has my lord called for me?" Esther asked, grateful for the warm admiration in Hegai's eyes.

"Yes, my lady. He said to bring you as soon as possible."

"Think of me," Esther murmured to Suhas. She wished she dared to say, "Pray for me." Would she ever be able to say those words to anyone again?

At the door of the banqueting room, Esther looked immediately for the king. He was perched on the edge of his throne like a small boy waiting for a promised surprise, watching the door. When Esther's eyes met his, he jumped to his feet, parted the curtain, and strode rapidly toward her.

"He never comes to meet anyone," Hegai whispered in a shocked tone.

Esther hardly heard him. She watched the king coming toward her. A narrow band of gold circled the linen cap that covered his dark head, and his robe, trousers, and patterned vest all glittered with jewels.

"My lord," Esther breathed and would have knelt, but he caught her hands and held her upright.

"Come," he said, his face proud.

She put her hand on his and walked beside him to the head table. There Ahasuerus faced the assembled people. A silence had fallen over the room, and every eye was on Esther. She had expected to be terrified, but the warmth of Ahasuerus's hand gave her courage.

"I present to you," Ahasuerus said loudly into the waiting silence, "your new queen—Queen Esther!"

She nodded her head graciously and heard the wave of sound that carried her name at its crest. Ahasuerus led her to the smaller of the two thrones and then sat beside her. For a few minutes it was impossible to talk, but when the crowd began to quiet down, Ahasuerus turned to her.

"You haven't even noticed the room," he said, disappointment in his voice.

"I have been hungry for the sight of you," she said truthfully. "When I have seen my king enough to satisfy my heart, then I'll look at the room."

His eyes warmed. "I'll be beside you most of the evening," he said, "so look at the room now."

She smiled and began to do as he instructed. In some strange way, it was as though she were seeing the room for the first time. It was important to her husband, she realized, that she be thrilled and awed. She had been when she saw the room with Suhas. And she still was.

When she turned back to Ahasuerus, she was breathless. "It's marvelous, my lord. The whole room is like a giant rose, glittering in the sunlight."

"How clever of you to see it," he cried. "That's exactly what the decorators had in mind, but they swore they had not told you."

"They hadn't. I'm overwhelmed, my lord."

He laughed with delight, and then commanded a servant to begin to serve them.

Esther joined in the pleasures of the evening, but one section of her mind was busy. She had let Ahasuerus see the amazement she'd felt when she first saw the room the day before. And it had made him happy. He had requested all this beauty to please her, she realized.

Her presence at the banquet was important to him. She would be sent back to her apartment, she knew, when the wilder entertainment was brought in to amuse the men. But for a little while Ahasuerus wanted her beside him.

I'll never like this sort of thing as much as he does, Esther thought as she took the pomegranate Ahasuerus was offering her. *But that doesn't matter.*

"You look as though someone had just given you a basket of gold," Ahasuerus observed.

"Something better than that," she answered. "I keep learning more and more about what it means to be married."

The king looked at her. "You don't really like lavish affairs like this, do you?" he said slowly. "You'd rather be quietly in your rooms."

"I'd rather be with you, my lord, than anywhere else in all the empire," she corrected. "That's what I just discovered. Being with you is what makes me happy."

He lifted her hand to his lips. "If you share the lavish events with me," he promised, "I'll see that we occasionally have quiet hours together. Is that fair?"

"Oh, my lord, more than fair!" she said and discovered, to her surprise, that she meant it with all her heart.

12

Plot in the Palace

"My lady!"

Esther was so absorbed in the scroll she was reading that she didn't look up. Even though she had been queen of the world's most powerful nation for three months now, she still had many days when nothing was demanded of her. Since it was unthinkable for a queen to work with her hands—and since she found the chatter and gossip of other women of the harem boring—she still spent much of her time reading.

Ahasuerus, she had discovered, was able to read but loathed it, so she had formed the habit of reading to him when he asked her. He liked the sound of her voice, he said. She had found that his agile mind was stimulated by the history, mythology, and even business items that she chose for him.

But today she was reading something she would not dare share with the king. In the last several batches of scrolls Hegai had brought to her, she had discovered portions of Jewish Scripture. Since she made a practice of keeping scrolls she particularly liked, no one was suspicious of the growing pile of Scripture on the shelves in her room. "The queen's library," the shelves were called, and no one cared which scrolls were there or how often she read them.

"My lady!" Suhas said again, louder this time.

"Oh, Suhas. Do you want something?"

"I have a message, my lady, from the old gatekeeper who means so much to you. He says that it's very important. He insists he must see you."

Esther stared at Suhas in astonishment. "See me? You mean, come to my apartment and talk to me?"

"Yes, my lady. He says it's terribly important."

Esther considered, frowning. She had waved to Mordecai many times from her window, and they had even exchanged notes once or twice. But he had never before asked to see her.

"I suppose I have the right to grant an audience," Esther said, "but I don't want to do anything that would cause gossip or displease the king." She looked at Suhas. "What should I do?"

"Do you want to see him, my lady?"

"Oh, of course." The words rushed out. "I'd love to see him. I just don't want to cause any trouble."

"Ask Hegai to usher him in, my lady, and to stay with you all the time the gatekeeper is here. Then it would be completely proper," Suhas explained.

In only a few minutes, Esther heard Mordecai's voice in the large sitting room. *I wish I could just run into his arms*, she thought, but she put the idea firmly from her. Until Mordecai decided it was safe, she had been forbidden to reveal their relationship to anyone. Queen or not, she still felt she ought to obey Mordecai.

She walked into the sitting room and watched Mordecai's eyes light up.

"My lady," he murmured and bent low before her.

"Come, my friend," she said quickly, not wanting him to bow to her. She pointed to a couch. "Will you sit here? I'm told you wanted to see me."

Hegai stayed close to the door, but she knew he would be able to hear every word. Mordecai sat where she told him to. It was obvious to Esther that he was very agitated.

"What is it? Are you in some kind of trouble? Do you need the ear of the king?"

Mordecai looked at her. "It's not me who's in trouble, my lady. It's the king who's in trouble."

Esther drew in her breath, aware of Hegai's abrupt movement. "What do you mean?" Esther's voice was sharper than she intended.

"May I tell my story from the beginning?" Mordecai asked. "Will you believe that what I tell you is true?"

"I would believe anything you said," Esther cried. "Just tell me quickly."

"You know I'm the keeper of the south gate," Mordecai began. "And you know that I'm faithful in my duties and never leave my post during my assigned hours."

"I know all that," Esther said impatiently. "Go on."

"Many people stop to rest in the shade of the gate," Mordecai continued. "They sit on the bench there and talk, and they don't pay any more attention to me than to the walls of the gate or the bench they sit on."

"So?" Esther prompted.

"So, two men who often go through my gate are Bigthan and Teresh."

The names meant nothing to Esther, but she saw a look of recognition on Hegai's face.

"Listen, my—friend," Esther said. "Is it all right if Hegai joins this conversation? He knows people and situations that I don't."

"If my lady trusts her servant," Mordecai said, "then, of course, I'll trust him, too."

Esther nodded at Hegai, who moved over to sit beside Mordecai.

"Do you know these men, Bigthan and Teresh?" Esther demanded.

Hegai nodded. "Yes, my lady. They're servants of the king. They ride with him when he goes hunting or into battle."

"That's why I didn't know them," Esther said. "All right, then, what about them?" she asked Mordecai.

"They sit and talk," Mordecai said. "They speak with ambition and greed. They seem to think they could profit if the king were dead."

"Dead?" The word was wrenched out of Esther with such horror that she thought perhaps the whole palace might have heard her.

Mordecai nodded, his eyes soft with compassion. "Yes, my lady, they're plotting against his life."

"I don't believe it," Hegai said stoutly. "They've been his faithful servants for years."

Esther had to force herself to be silent a moment, lest she say too much in Mordecai's defense. Finally she was able to say mildly, "I've known Mordecai for years, Hegai. He has never lied to anyone. Why would he start now?"

"What did you hear?" Hegai asked.

"They talked about setting up another king who would give them greater power than they have now."

"Do you know what their plans are?" Esther asked.

"Yes. Teresh, who is a favorite of the king, will discover that the king's taster is ill. They plan to feed the taster contaminated food to assure it. The discovery won't be made until a few minutes before the king dines tonight.

"Teresh will take the place of the taster. He'll pretend to sip the wine—he's very clever at sleight of hand—and he'll approve the wine which the king will drink. The wine will be poisoned!"

Esther's mind was reeling, but she caught one word. "Tonight, you say?" she cried. "They plan to do this tonight?"

Mordecai's face was grim. "Tonight."

Esther was silent a moment, and then she turned to Mordecai. "Thank you," she said formally. She could only hope that he would see the appreciation in her eyes, even though her words had to be stilted. "I'm more grateful than I can say. You can be sure that somehow we'll prevent this terrible thing from happening. And the king will know that it was you who saved his life."

Mordecai stood. "I'll leave, so you can make your plans. Thank you for listening, my lady."

Impulsively, she reached up and took Mordecai's hand in hers. "Go in peace," she said and then turned abruptly to Hegai. "Go to the king," she commanded. "Tell him—no, ask him—if he will come to my room. Tell him I'll take only a minute of his time. Tell him it's of the greatest importance."

"He may laugh, my lady," Hegai warned.

"Tell him it's a matter of life or death," she implored. "Tell him it's *my* life that's in danger."

"But that's not true," Hegai protested.

"Yes, it is. Do you think I could go on living if he were dead?"

Hegai stared at Esther for a minute and then moved toward the door. "I'll tell him," he said. "But I can't promise he'll come."

13

A Cup of Poison

Ahasuerus threw back his head and roared with laughter. "You expect me to believe that?" he cried.

"My lord, it's true." Esther's hands were gripped tightly together, and she was on the verge of tears.

"And how am I to be killed?" Ahasuerus asked, as though to humor her.

"Please don't mock me, my lord. You're to be given poisoned wine tonight when you're eating supper."

"And my taster?" Ahasuerus's voice was still teasing.

"He won't be there. They've planned to feed him spoiled food so that he'll be too sick to serve you. One of the murderers will take his place."

"Do you think just anyone could serve as my taster?"

There was scorn in Ahasuerus's voice. "Don't you suppose I'd insist that it be someone I could trust?"

"Of course, my lord. But this man *is* someone you trust."

Ahasuerus became very still. "What are you trying to say? Are you suggesting that Haman . . . ?"

Esther let her mind touch briefly on the thin, cold face of the man who seemed to be gaining more and more power in her husband's realm. She felt her flesh crawl every time she was near Haman. It was only natural, since he was an Amalekite. She had never forgotten the day the Amalekites had killed her family. She wished for one fervent second that it was, indeed, Haman who was the villain of this plot.

"No," she said, "it isn't Haman. It's someone else, my lord. I—wish I didn't have to tell you."

"Who?" Ahasuerus's voice was harsh.

"Bigthan and Teresh, my lord," she admitted reluctantly.

Once again, Ahasuerus's head tipped back while his laughter filled the room. "Oh, come," he said. "That's ridiculous. They're two of my most faithful men."

"You've *got* to believe me." Her voice was thin with her desperation. "It's true. The man who brought the story to Hegai and me is completely honest. You've got to get rid of Bigthan and Teresh at once."

"Without even a trial?" The king's voice was silky. "No, it's best to let them go ahead with their plans," he said. At her look of terror, he smiled. "Never fear, little one. I'll be very careful, and if it goes as you say—"

His voice slowed and she saw the firm set of his jaw. She had heard of the king's ruthlessness when he was angry, but she had never seen any indication of it until now.

"And if it goes as I've said?" she prompted.

"They will both die. Hanged on a gibbet," Ahasuerus said coldly.

"What if they try another plan and you're not properly warned?" she whispered in a trembling voice.

"Would it matter so much to you?" he asked.

"Oh, my lord," she began, but could not find the words.

Ahasuerus sat studying her for a minute, and then with a sudden laugh, gathered her into his arms. "Don't worry," he said. "You've warned me and so nothing can take me by surprise. I'll come to you when the thing is settled, and tell you everything that happens. Will that do?"

"It will have to." Her voice caught and she swallowed. "I'll be waiting, my lord." *And praying*, she added to herself.

He stood up and smiled at her with the fond look one would give to a child. "You know, of course," he said in a casual voice, "that I don't believe any of it. I'll only be watchful to please you."

"Yes, my lord," she said and watched him leave the room with a feeling of dread.

As soon as he was gone, she ran to her shelves and pulled out one of the scrolls of Jewish Scripture she had hoarded. Unrolling it feverishly, she scanned the words, seeking the ones she needed. Her lips trembled, reading the words of King David. "The Lord is my shepherd; I shall lack nothing."

The words were like a healing oil on her troubled

heart. She went on reading until she found the particular words she had been seeking. "Even though I walk through the valley of the shadow of death, I will fear no evil, for you are with me."

For the first time in her life, she understood Mordecai's feeling about Yahweh, the God who loves his people as a shepherd loves his sheep. She knew she needed God's help desperately now.

Clutching the scroll in her hands, Esther lifted her face upwards. "Oh, Yahweh, my God," she whispered. "Thank you for letting Uncle Mordecai overhear this dreadful plan, so that I could warn my husband. Surely, my God, this must mean that you want the king's life spared." Her voice quivered and she resorted to the plain words of a child. "Oh, please, *please*, don't let anything happen to him!"

The hours of late afternoon and early evening crawled by. Esther tried to read, but the words blurred in front of her eyes. At Suhas's suggestion, she went out into the walled garden and tried to walk along the paths bordered with roses. There had been comfort for her before in the fragrance and privacy of the little yard, but today she felt fenced in by the walls, smothered by the scent of the flowers. For all she knew, Ahasuerus might be lying dead beside his chair. He had been so casual about her warning, and the plotters were obviously clever.

She ran back to her room, not even waiting for an escort. When Suhas came looking for her, Esther was pacing rapidly back and forth from window to door, her hands clenched into tight fists.

"Let me bring you a light supper," Suhas offered.

"How can I eat?" Esther retorted. "I'd choke on the food."

"A glass of wine, my lady? Perhaps a bit of milk?"

"Just leave me alone!" The words were snapped out before Esther could stop them. Immediately she turned to Suhas with an apology. "I'm sorry, Suhas. It's not your fault. But I can't stand this not knowing."

"I understand, my lady. Would you like me to go to the other end of the palace to see if I can learn anything?"

"Oh, would you?"

Suhas nodded and turned to leave the room. But just at that moment, Esther's door opened and a slave came in, followed by Ahasuerus.

With a glad cry, Esther jumped up and ran toward the king. "You're all right! You're really all right."

"Of course," Ahasuerus said, but his face was grim. He made a sign to his slave and to Suhas. "Go," he commanded, "and leave us alone."

His voice was so harsh that Esther felt a sinking sensation in her chest. Had Mordecai been misled, and had her warning been a foolish thing? Was the king angry because she had raised suspicion against his loyal servants?

When the door closed behind the slave, Ahasuerus took Esther in his arms. "If it weren't for you," he said hoarsely, "I would be lying dead on the floor of the dining hall."

"Oh, my lord." She put her arms around his waist and held on fiercely.

After a few seconds, he pushed her gently away from

him. "Sit down," he said. "I'll tell you everything."

Trembling, she sat on the edge of the couch and watched the king stride angrily back and forth across the room.

"It happened just as you said it would. Only a few minutes before my meal was served, word came from the kitchen that my taster had taken ill and could not serve me. I reacted in a normal fashion by requesting that one of my faithful followers take his place. Someone I could trust completely."

He took another swift turn around the room. "Everyone agreed that Teresh was the logical choice. Was anyone in the kingdom more faithful? Did anyone love the king more?"

He stopped and smacked one fist into the other palm. "I would have staked my life on it," he said bitterly. "If anyone had asked me to name a loyal man, I would have named Haman first and Teresh second. That's what cuts so deeply."

Esther nodded. "If it had been an enemy, you would have felt only anger, no pain."

"Exactly." He resumed his striding. "I pretended to be delighted, and I wasn't completely pretending. I still found the thing hard to believe, even when everything was going as you had predicted."

She sat very still, watching, listening, and all the time her heart was singing a hymn of praise to her God.

"When the wine was served, Teresh tasted it. I could have sworn he tasted it. The man should have been a magician instead of a soldier. I took the glass from him and started to tip it to my lips."

"Oh, no," Esther breathed.

Ahasuerus glanced at her, his face softening for a moment. Then he continued his story, and his look of anger returned. "At the last second, I hesitated. I said I wanted my friend, Teresh, to have the best of the wine. If he was willing to risk his life for me, it was the least I could do."

"What did he say?"

"He refused, of course. He pretended that it was out of love for me. But I continued to press him, almost forcing his fingers around the cup. When I made him lift it to his lips, he finally broke and would have flung the cup away."

"And spilled the proof," Esther interrupted shrewdly.

Ahasuerus stopped again and stared at her. "You're the most amazing girl," he announced. "Your mind works like a man's."

She didn't respond except to lean forward and beg, "Go on."

"I snatched the cup away and prevented him from spilling the wine, but when I would have forced it to his lips, he began to grovel and beg. It was disgusting."

After another short silence, the king said coldly, "It would have been better if he had drunk the wine. Death from poison is quicker and easier than death on the gibbet."

She drew a shuddering breath. "What about the other man—what was his name?"

"Bigthan was already in custody, and poison was found on him when he was searched. They died together. All who hear of this affair will be warned of the consequences of plotting against the king."

Esther let out her breath in relief. "I suppose I ought to feel some pity for them, but I can only feel thankful that their horrible plan failed. I don't know what I would have done—" Her voice trailed off, and she looked with suddenly brimming eyes at her husband.

Ahasuerus came over to her, and took her hands gently in his. "You asked me once if I could learn to love you," he said. "I suppose, in a way, I have always loved you, ever since that night you first tried to juggle those colored balls. But today, seeing your pain at what might have happened to me . . . You needn't ever wonder now whether or not I love you, little one."

She smiled up at him through her tears. "The most important thing is that you're safe," she finally said.

Ahasuerus bent down and kissed her forehead. "Now," he said, "it's time for you to tell me who your informant was. And how did he know of the plot against me?"

She told her story carefully, revealing only that Mordecai was an old friend and the man who had taught her to read. She explained how he had overheard the plans, and Ahasuerus listened with the same concentration he gave all important matters.

"And his name is Mordecai, you say?" he asked when she had finished.

"Yes, my lord. Mordecai. He's a gatekeeper at the south gate."

Ahasuerus raised his voice and called to the slave who waited outside the door. "Go to my scribe," he ordered. "Tell him to make note that on this day a certain Mordecai, keeper of the south gate, saved the life of the king. Mark it down carefully so that proper reward can be made to him at a convenient time."

"Yes, my lord," the slave said, starting to back from the room.

"Perhaps I ought to have Haman write it down," Ahasuerus mused.

Esther spoke with breathless haste. "Oh, no, my lord, don't bother Haman with such an ordinary task." *Why am I so sure,* she asked herself, *that if Haman knew Mordecai was a Jew, he would somehow distort the facts?* "Your first idea to have the scribe do it is wise, I think."

Ahasuerus settled himself comfortably among the cushions. He gave a careless little wave of his hand. "It doesn't matter. Perhaps Queen Esther is right and I shouldn't trouble Haman with such a minor task. Go, tell the scribe, boy. Don't just stand there."

The slave scuttled out of the room as Ahasuerus turned to Esther. "Read something to me," he said. "I want to forget the treachery of this day."

She reached into her pile for a scroll that she knew contained an amusing tale. "Of course, my lord. Here, rest your head on this cushion. Now, shall I begin?"

I should be the happiest woman in all the world, Esther thought, rolling open the scroll. *Instead, I'm filled with uneasiness. Teresh and Bigthan plotted to kill the king, and were foiled, but I know that in a palace there is always treachery and plotting. How can I even guess what terrible things tomorrow may hold?*

14

The Amalekite

Esther, sitting at the king's side, looked around the table. Only rarely was she invited to have dinner with Ahasuerus and his guests, but when Ahasuerus wanted her with him, she always obeyed.

The king suddenly raised his cup toward Haman. "Our gathering tonight is to celebrate Haman's latest promotion," he said, laughing.

Esther saw the surprise and greed on Haman's face. Even when she tried not to dislike the man simply because he was an Amalekite, she could not rid herself of an uneasy feeling about him. She sensed a ruthless ambition in Haman and wished that Ahasuerus could see it, too. But the king was charmed with Haman's cleverness and his willingness to perform any task.

"My promotion?" Haman asked, his voice shaking with sudden excitement. "I haven't heard of any promotion."

"How could you?" Ahasuerus said with lazy affection. "I've only just now decided on it. When I saw how skillfully you arranged the last collection of taxes, I knew you had to be rewarded. And now I've decided what the reward should be."

If Haman were a dog, he'd be panting and wagging his tail, Esther thought with scorn, looking at his flushed face.

"You've been so clever at everything I've asked you to do, so faithful in every way, that I've decided you're to be made the grand emir, second only to me in the ruling of my kingdom." Ahasuerus's voice was as casual as if he were giving away a toy.

For a few seconds, Haman seemed stunned. "My lord," he stuttered. "I never expected such an honor. I never knew—"

"Well, you know it now," Ahasuerus said. "I'll have an edict sent out at once that you, and only you, will have the power to make decisions and rules. Aside from me, of course. But you know I don't have time to visit all the lands under my rule or investigate all the problems. Other than clearing certain actions with me, you'll have freedom to do as you please."

Esther felt her uneasiness grow as Haman's face became more and more inflamed with his importance.

My husband is wrong, she thought with dismay. *Haman is greedy and selfish and ruthless. I'm not at all sure he can be trusted, and if he knew I was a Jew . . .* Her thoughts had circled around to the true core of her distrust of Haman. As an Amalekite, he had doubtlessly been taught since infancy to hate the Jews. Even though she was married to Ahasuerus, that would not change the fact that he would think of her as his enemy if he learned her true nationality. And then he might even try to turn the king against her.

"Will all the people be told about this, my lord?" Haman asked. "Will they know that they ought to bow to me because of my high position?" His voice was eager.

"Why not? As grand emir, you'll rank higher than anyone else. I'll put that in the edict, too. I'll say that everyone is to bow before you. There, does that please you?"

"Oh, yes, my lord." Haman's face showed streaks of perspiration, and Esther's disgust and fear increased.

"Well, then," Ahasuerus said, glancing at Esther and evidently seeing some of her emotions on her face, "it's settled. With the exception of me, and of course my queen, all others will bow to you. Now," he called to the slaves, "bring on the dancers and the musicians. Let's have only merriment in this room. No long faces!"

The last command was meant for Esther, she knew, although he did not humiliate her by using her name. Obediently, she smiled at her husband, but fear and dread made a cold, hollow feeling in the pit of her stomach.

As the months went by after the king had singled out Haman for promotion, there was much talk of Haman's growing power. Esther heard some of the gossip and her fear of the man increased.

"He demands that everyone bow to the floor before him," Suhas reported one day. "Even women here in the palace, those of us who pass him in the halls a dozen times a day."

Esther saw that the girl's hands were trembling, and she felt a sense of foreboding. Suhas was not usually shaken from her composure.

"We've never had to do anything more than bob in a sort of curtsy here in the palace," Suhas went on. "If I were to meet any of the king's officers outside the walls, I'd bow to the ground. But this morning, when I passed the grand emir, Haman, in the halls and gave only a small bow, he called me back and—and forced me to my knees."

"Forced you?" Esther asked coldly. "You mean he laid hands on you? You belong to me."

"He slapped me, my lady." Suhas looked apologetic. "I think he was very angry about something. Maybe someone else had failed to bow."

Esther's voice got still colder. "I won't stand for it. He has no right to slap my slaves, especially you. Even the king knows that you are as much my friend as you are my slave."

"Thank you, my lady," Suhas murmured.

"Don't worry. It won't happen again," Esther said grimly.

"You mustn't say anything about it," Suhas begged. "You might make the king very angry. I've learned my lesson, my lady. From now on, I'll bow to the ground for the grand emir, no matter where I meet him."

"Nevertheless," Esther insisted, "I intend to say

something at the first opportunity. Either I am queen or I am not."

And nothing Suhas could say made her change her mind.

Several days later, Esther and Ahasuerus sat together in her room, sharing one of their few times of privacy.

"Read to me," Ahasuerus said, stretching out his legs. "I'm tired of the talk of men. Read something gentle and romantic."

She thought of the songs which King Solomon had written to his bride and wondered if she dared read them to the king. But first she intended to voice her displeasure over Haman's treatment of Suhas.

"Of course I'll read to you, my lord, but first I want to make a complaint."

His face lost its sleepy look immediately. "What do you mean, 'complaint'?" he barked. "What does a woman dare complain about?"

"I've never complained before, my lord. You're generous beyond belief. But something has upset me."

"What? Has anyone been disrespectful to you?"

"In a way," she admitted. "Your grand emir, Haman, has mistreated my favorite slave—slapping her and forcing her to grovel before him. I don't like it."

He narrowed his eyes and stared at her. "You don't like it, eh? Well, there's nothing to be done about it. I've given Haman the right to do as he pleases. How would it seem if I went running to him with every little complaint that came my way?"

"But I'm your wife, my lord." Her voice was cold and stiff.

"And Haman is my second in command," he shot

back, the words as cold and stiff as hers.

"I thought that, as queen, I had *some* voice," she said.

"You're a *woman,*" he shouted at her. "If it weren't for my kindness, you could be a slave scrubbing floors."

"Yes, my lord," she said, but there was no apology in her tone. She heard how surly her voice was, but she couldn't seem to change it.

Ahasuerus stood up. "You're no better than any other woman," he said bitterly. "Whining, sniveling, demanding special favors."

He paused as though giving her an opportunity to run to him with apology and love. But she stubbornly averted her eyes. *He has chosen Haman over me,* she thought. *If that's the way he wants it—*

Ahasuerus spun on his heel. "I don't care if I never see you again!" he shot over his shoulder as he stamped out of the room.

For a few minutes more, her fury sustained her, but then she began to realize just what she had done. She had angered the king of Persia, the most powerful man in the world. He had only to say the word, and she could be sent away in disgrace or even killed, and replaced by another girl from the harem.

And for what? Because she distrusted and feared Haman. She had felt no real anger against Ahasuerus. She had been jealous and spiteful, wanting her husband to humiliate Haman for her sake.

She should have known better. No man, least of all a king, would reprimand his best friend for the sake of a woman. She had been foolish. Dangerously foolish. The king had discarded Vashti because he had been angry with her. Might he not do the same to Esther?

Putting her hands over her face, Esther started to weep, and even Suhas, when she came in later, could not comfort her or ease her grief.

A month went by, and during that time, Esther neither saw nor heard from King Ahasuerus. The days seemed to drag from morning until night, and Esther lived in constant dread that the king would punish her for her arrogance.

Suhas listened to every bit of gossip she could gather in the palace, and reported to Esther that no one even mentioned that Ahasuerus no longer called Esther to his rooms.

However, there was another very disquieting piece of news which Suhas brought one day. She had heard that Mordecai, the keeper of the south gate, had stubbornly refused to bow to Haman.

"Oh, no," Esther breathed when she heard it. "He wouldn't be so foolish."

"Ator tells me that he has heard several people talking about it. It seems this man, Mordecai, is a Jew. Had you known that, my lady?"

"Everyone in Shushan is something," Esther said lightly. "Mede or Persian or Egyptian or Jew."

"Or Indian," Suhas added with a smile. "Well, anyhow, I guess the grand emir hates Jews and is furious with the gatekeeper. But nothing will make Mordecai bend his neck."

Esther felt despair building up in her heart, but there was nothing she could do. She no longer had the ear of the king, and she could not go openly to Mordecai and beg him to humble himself. Even if she wrote to him, she was sure he would ignore her advice. Mordecai could be even more stubborn than she.

"Do you think Haman will kill him?" Esther asked, her voice trembling.

"I asked Ator," Suhas said. "He said it would be unseemly for the grand emir to have a simple gatekeeper killed for such a small offense. But he—Ator, that is—said that Haman was very angry. No one knows what he'll do, but I'm sure your friend is in great danger, my lady."

It's my fault, Esther mourned inside her heart. *If I had been wiser and more discreet, the king would not be angry with me. My own pride and stubbornness have created this danger for my beloved Mordecai. Oh, Yahweh, what can I do?*

15

For Such a Time as This

For the next few days, Esther suffered greater loneliness than she had ever known. Ahasuerus continued to ignore her, and her worry over what might happen to Mordecai tormented her constantly.

One afternoon, Suhas came to Esther's room. "Are you willing to see Hathach, my lady?" she asked.

Hathach, the eunuch who served Esther along with Hegai, had, like Hegai and Suhas, been respecting Esther's grief and leaving her alone. If he had asked for an audience, he must have good reason.

"Of course," she said listlessly.

"I'm sorry he must bring additional worries to you, my lady."

"Additional worries for me?"

"Hathach will explain," Suhas said and disappeared through the door.

"My lady." Hathach bent his head in humility, though there was no need for Esther's servants to grovel before her, and they knew it. "My lady, I bring you a message from the gatekeeper, Mordecai."

Her heart twisted with sudden fear. Had Mordecai's stubbornness brought him into real danger? "Yes, Hathach, tell me quickly," she said, holding her voice steady.

"He sent you this, my lady." Hathach placed a sheet of paper in her hand.

She glanced at it quickly and saw at once that it bore the name of Haman, the grand emir, but that it was signed with the seal of the king's own ring. She read the paper with growing horror. At last she lifted her head and looked at Hathach.

"Do you know about this?"

"Yes, my lady. Hegai insisted that the edict be kept from you, because of your friendship with Mordecai. Did you know he was a Jew, my lady?" Without waiting for her to answer, he went on agitatedly. "But Hegai's away from the palace today, so I couldn't resist when Mordecai begged me to bring you a copy of the edict."

"Of course not," she said, pushing the words past the cold lump of fear in her throat. "I should have been told even sooner."

"Yes, my lady," Hathach mumbled.

"All the Jews," she whispered. "*All* the Jews. The edict says that all the Jews are to be killed on the thirteenth of the month of Adar. Even women and children," she added, her voice shaking.

"Yes, my lady. And all their possessions seized. The grand emir, Haman, made the suggestion to the king some days ago. He promised to pay ten thousand silver talents into the king's treasury, I understand, and so the king gave his own ring to be used to seal the edict."

"No doubt the ten thousand talents are to be stolen from the Jews," Esther interrupted bitterly.

"No doubt, my lady. The edict has already been sent out to every province that is under the king's rule. You know that such edicts are final and cannot be changed, my lady."

"Well, then, what does Mordecai expect me to do?" she wailed. "Haman would never listen to a word I said."

"Mordecai asked that you go to the king," Hathach reported. "He said surely you could persuade the king."

Esther stared at him, stricken. "How can I? I haven't been called into the king's presence for thirty days. And if I went into his chamber without an invitation from him, you know what could happen."

"Yes, my lady." Hathach's voice was nearly as shaken as hers. "Unless he raised his golden scepter toward you—"

"And the king is angry at me," Esther whispered. "He would not raise the scepter. Go and tell Mordecai that. Tell him I'll be killed if I go before the king."

"Yes, my lady. I'll go at once. He's outside the palace gate, dressed in sackcloth and smeared with ashes. It's why he didn't come to you himself, my lady. No one is allowed in the palace compound in sackcloth."

Esther quickly turned her face so that Hathach

would not see her tears. "Please," she said in a muffled voice, "please see that he has a new robe to wear, something clean and decent. And take him my answer quickly."

"Yes, my lady. I'll be back as soon as I can."

While Hathach was gone, Esther walked the floor of her sitting room, twisting her hands together. A thousand times she had regretted her hasty words to Ahasuerus, but there was no way now to unsay what had been said. She made and rejected a dozen plans while she waited, but there seemed to be no solution. If she went to the king, she would die. If she did not go, Mordecai would die.

"Oh, Yahweh," she whispered. "Show me what to do. Give me courage to do the right thing."

Almost immediately, Hathach was at her door. "My lady," he said hesitantly, "may I come in?"

"Of course. What did he say?"

Hathach looked perplexed. "He said, my lady, that you could not escape any more than any other Jew."

In spite of the danger, Esther felt a great sense of relief. This was the time, then, to admit she was a Jew, that she was Mordecai's relative, that Yahweh was their God. She nodded to Hathach. "He's right, of course. I'm as Jewish as he is. He's my uncle."

Hathach looked stunned. "Would the king have permitted such an edict if he had known, my lady?"

"I don't know," she admitted. "I hope not, but for all I know, the king might . . . welcome my death."

"Oh, no, my lady!" Hathach protested, but she cut across the words.

"Is that all my uncle said?"

"No, my lady. He said if you stayed aloof from this tragedy, that your father's family would perish. He said, my lady, that it may be for such a time as this that you were brought to be queen."

She stood very still. She remembered her reluctance to enter the king's contest years before, Mordecai's confidence that she could win, and his prayers to Yahweh. She remembered also how she had run away when the Amalekites attacked their caravan from Babylon. She thought of all the times she had run away from difficulties by burying herself in her reading. And she remembered the promise she had made to herself—that she would never run away again.

She lifted her head. "Tell my uncle," she said clearly, "to gather all the Jews of Shushan together and to fast and pray for three days. Tell him my servants and I will do the same."

She paused for a second, and Hathach spoke eagerly. "We'll do anything to help. Hegai will be home tonight, and I know he'll join in such a fast."

"Then tell my uncle," Esther said resolutely, "that I will do as he asks. He knows that I'll be breaking the law if I go uninvited to my lord, the king. But if I die, I die."

Hathach's lips trembled. "Oh, my lady," he began.

"No, don't waste time to pity me. Go and tell my uncle that I've agreed and that I have portions of our sacred Scripture to read and comfort me. Tell him—" Her courage began to fray. "Tell him to pray for me."

Hathach bowed and left. After he was gone, Esther moved over to her couch and knelt beside it. "Oh,

Yahweh, my God," she whispered, "move the king's heart to pity. Make him look at me with love."

For three days, Esther fasted and prayed, meditated, and read the Scripture. During the daylight hours, she did not even take water, and although she encouraged her servants to eat something in the evening, she herself did not touch food. She had expected to suffer from hunger or to become very weak. But she was so lifted up by the strength from Yahweh that seemed to flow through her that she did not even think of eating.

She thought often of Mordecai and the other Jews of Shushan. In some strange way, they seemed closer to her than her own skin. There was absolutely no doubt in her mind that they, too, were calling on the Most High God, asking for strength and courage for the queen who would have to risk her life for them.

On the last morning, she woke, and almost immediately the plan she had been seeking began to take shape in her mind.

"Yahweh has given me a plan," she confided to Suhas. "Now, help me dress so that I will be as beautiful as possible."

"Yes, my lady." Suhas's eyes were red-rimmed from weeping. "Do you want to wear the plain robes you usually wear?"

"My lord Ahasuerus has found them fair in the past," Esther said, and could not prevent the catch in her voice. "The heavy ivory silk robe, I think, with the blue girdle. And the gold bracelets and anklets he has given me. He likes—he used to like my hair braided."

"Yes, my lady. And I'll never stop praying while you're gone."

"Praying?"

"To your God, Yahweh," Suhas said shyly. "He has given you such courage and grace, my lady, that I know he must love you. Surely he will hear even me."

Esther leaned forward and kissed her friend's cheek. "Thank you," she said, and could say no more.

An hour later, Suhas handed the metal mirror to her mistress. "Is everything all right, my lady?" Her voice trembled.

Esther stared at her reflected face. Suhas's work was skillfully done, but that was no guarantee that Ahasuerus would look at her with love. She managed a wooden nod of assurance. "You've done everything that can possibly be done, Suhas," she whispered and tried to smile.

Suhas's voice was low but intent. "Not everything, my lady. I haven't tried to persuade you not to risk your life."

Esther looked at the girl in astonishment, and Suhas's face went crimson.

"Oh, I know I have no right, my lady. And I know you have much faith in your God—so much that even I am trying not to be afraid. But do you remember Arla, my lady? That insolent minx from Egypt? She was so sure that the king was in love with her after her visit with him that she went unannounced to his royal chamber, and—"

"And?" Esther prompted as the girl's voice trailed off.

"He was very busy that morning, my lady. And in a

very bad mood. They had no trouble persuading him the girl should be killed."

Esther stood still, staring at Suhas. "They?" she asked in a whisper.

"Haman and the others," Suhas answered. "No one really liked her, my lady, even though she was very beautiful."

Esther felt the icy clutch of fear in her stomach. For a few seconds she stood rigid and cold. Then she remembered something that Mordecai had told her when she had first come to live with him, and her nightmares had jerked her awake screaming in the middle of the night.

"Yahweh doesn't always take away your fear," he had said, "but he gives you the strength to bear it."

Well, then, she couldn't expect to walk to Ahasuerus without fear. But, with Yahweh's help, she could walk. That was all that mattered. Turning, she put her hand lightly on the arm of Hegai, who stood waiting. "Take me to the royal chamber," she said.

They walked the long corridors in silence, and Esther's heart pounded in her ears. Would she ever walk these halls again? Would she ever see sunshine, or hear birds sing, or read a scroll?

Her hand on Hegai's arm began to tremble violently. *I don't even have a definite plan to save the Jews,* she thought with growing panic. *I have only this feeling that Yahweh will show me a plan. But what if he doesn't? Haman is powerful and clever and wicked. What woman could possibly defeat him? Especially since the king's edict has already gone out and cannot be recalled!*

"I'm too young to die!" To her horror, she had said the words out loud.

Hegai put his strong, warm fingers over her trembling hand. "It's not too late, my lady," he whispered. "We can turn the next corner in the corridor and go back to your room another way. It may be that we can keep the king unaware of the fact that you're a Jew."

For a minute, the temptation and the fear were almost too great for her to bear. Then, resolutely, she pushed them out of her mind. Uncle Mordecai was right. Yahweh had surely brought her here for such a time as this. She only had to trust him.

"No," she said firmly.

At the entrance to the royal chamber, Hegai looked at her once with affection before he pushed open the door.

"The lady Esther," he cried in a loud voice, "come to seek an audience with the king."

Esther saw everyone in the room turn to look at her with astonishment. She could hear the sound of indrawn breath, and she could almost feel the fear that filled the air.

But she looked only toward the king. He had raised his head at the sound of Hegai's voice and was looking across the room at Esther.

Oh, Yahweh, please! she thought. She lifted her head and felt her lips curving into a smile as she looked into Ahasuerus's eyes.

16

Touch of the Golden Scepter

For a moment, Ahasuerus didn't move. Then, while Esther held her breath, he stooped to pick up the golden scepter and point it toward her.

"Will the lady Esther approach and speak to the king?" the servant beside the throne called out as soon as the scepter began to rise.

Esther's knees shook so badly that she was grateful for Hegai's arm as they moved across the room. At the throne, she reached out to touch the tip of the scepter, then knelt gracefully and bent her head. In just a few seconds, she felt Ahasuerus's hands lifting her to her feet, and she dared to look up into his face.

"What is troubling you, Queen Esther?"

Her heart began to race. *Queen.* With that simple word, he had returned her to her place of honor and prestige. And he did it in front of everyone in his chamber. He could so easily have said just her name, or "Lady Esther." But the deliberate use of her royal title made all the difference.

"I wanted to speak to the king," she said quietly, but she was sure her heart was in her eyes.

"Anything you want," he said quickly. "Anything up to half of my kingdom is yours if you ask it."

She risked a smile. How often she had told him that his impulsive generosity might get him into serious trouble someday.

"Nothing like that, my lord," she answered. "I want only for my lord and his servant Haman to dine in my apartment tonight."

She saw the surprise and pleasure on the king's face. She was sure he was thinking that at last she had come to her senses about Haman.

"I can speak for Haman, I think, when I say that we will be delighted to come. Two hours before sunset?"

"Two hours before sunset, my lord."

He spoke very softly. "Then I'll work all day to hurry the sun across the sky."

Her smile was genuine. "And I, my lord."

Bowing, she backed away from the vicinity of the throne. Hegai stepped up to meet her, and together they left the royal chamber.

In the hall, Hegai looked at her curiously. "I thought you meant to speak of Mordecai, my lady."

"When I know the king loves me again, then I'll speak of Mordecai and of all the Jews." Her voice was steady but her heart was singing. With the king to support her, to love her, there was every possibility that the Jews would not die.

That evening, Esther wore a simple robe of deep blue silk, girdled with a narrow cord of gold. Suhas braided a thin gold cord into her dark hair, and slender gold bracelets shone on her wrists.

"I remember thinking once that it wasn't important to be beautiful," Esther said, holding the metal mirror up to examine Suhas's work. "Now I know how important it is for me to please the king. Is everything ready? Have Hegai and Hathach taken care of everything?"

"Yes, my lady. There is roast lamb and lentils fixed with oil, and melons, pomegranates, and grapes. And bread, of course, and wine. All of it prepared with skill."

"And the table set with the finest dishes?"

"Of course, my lady. The king's cup will be from his own table."

The words were hard to say, but Esther forced them out. "And my lord Haman? There's a rich cup for him?"

Suhas's eyes met her mistress's squarely. "A cup of beaten gold, my lady." The words were toneless.

"Good." Esther hesitated a minute. "You'll have to trust me, Suhas. I can't tell you exactly what I'm going to do, because I'm not sure myself. I only know that Yahweh will reveal his plan to me as the hours go by."

"Yes, my lady. I know you haven't invited Haman out of affection."

Esther heard voices in the hall. "They're coming," she said in a choked voice. "I'll go to meet them."

As she entered the sitting room, she saw with pleasure that Ahasuerus and Haman were both dressed as though attending a royal banquet. The king wore his crown and Haman his best robe in honor of her, she realized, and so she was able to relax and greet them with less worry.

The evening moved along more pleasantly than she had dared hope. After the excellent meal, the entertainment which she had provided seemed to delight her guests. She had requested jugglers, and she met Ahasuerus's eyes when the balls were tossed lightly, deftly into the air.

"You remember," he whispered under cover of the music.

"Of course, my lord," she smiled.

Later, when the entertainment had ended, Ahasuerus asked Esther to tell them one of the stories she had read. She had suspected this might happen and so was prepared.

"I've discovered there are many stories of courage," she said, "but one which moved me a great deal is a story of an ancient flood."

"Everyone knows the world was once destroyed by flood," Haman said. "I've often wondered how anyone survived it."

"There was a man," Esther began in a soft, storytelling voice. "A man whose name was Noah. He was a good and righteous man."

She saw a quick flicker of suspicion on Haman's face, but she kept her voice gentle and impersonal.

Skillfully, she painted a word picture of the god (she never named Yahweh) who commanded that Noah build an ark. She told of Noah's obedience, the gathering of the animals in pairs, of the rain that did not stop for forty days. She described the howling winds, the raging waters, and the desolation that followed.

Then, softening her voice, she told of the dove bringing the sprig from the olive tree to show that new life had begun on earth. She lifted her hands as if to trace the pastel rainbow that had curved across the sky.

"The rainbow, then, is a promise," she explained. "A promise that Noah's god would never destroy the world with a flood again."

She stopped and smiled at the two men.

"It's a charming tale," Haman said, "and the queen is a marvelous storyteller."

"Noah's god is fascinating," Ahasuerus mused. "He can be angry enough to destroy a world of evil men, and loving enough to save one good man's family. I could worship such a god, I think."

"Many people do, my lord," Esther murmured. But she was thinking of the rainbow thrown across the sky. Yahweh kept his promises. He had promised Noah that the world would not be destroyed in a flood.

He had also promised Abraham, the father of the Jews, that his descendants would number as the stars. Yahweh would not let them be destroyed now—even by Haman and the royal edict.

"But come," the king insisted, breaking into her thoughts. "Surely you had a reason for wanting to talk to me. This has all been very nice, but if you have a request, feel free to make it. As I told you earlier, I would give you anything you wanted, even to half of my kingdom."

Esther bowed her head. "My lord, I ask only one thing. If this evening has been pleasant, I beg for another. If the king and his servant Haman would visit me again tomorrow—"

The king creased his brow, then shrugged and smiled indulgently. Haman appeared feverishly eager.

"Why not?" Ahasuerus said lazily. "Would it suit you, Haman?"

"I'm honored," Haman almost babbled. "The queen is gracious to me."

"Then, my lord," Esther announced, "I'll count the hours until you return tomorrow."

It was so obviously a dismissal that both men rose at once. They expressed their gratitude again, and Ahasuerus let Haman leave the room first, so that he could speak privately to Esther.

"You're lovelier than I remembered," he said.

"And you, my lord, are more generous than I deserve." She longed to run into his arms, but she knew—and was not sure how she knew—that this was not the right time for that.

Ahasuerus hesitated, then swung on his heel and left the room.

Taking a deep breath, Esther moved over to the window. She gazed up at the brilliance of the stars. "Oh, Yahweh, my Lord," she breathed, "open the king's heart still wider."

Suhas woke Esther early the next morning. "My lady," she breathed. "Wake up."

Esther blinked in surprise at this unusual intrusion. Usually she was allowed to sleep as long as she liked.

"Is there something wrong?"

"Not wrong, my lady. But the most incredible gossip is going through the palace."

Esther pushed herself up until she was sitting against her pillows. "What is it?"

"Last night," Suhas said in a voice that shook with excitement, "the grand emir, Haman, was so puffed up over being invited to your apartment that he thought nothing in the world could bring him down. But when he left the palace, Mordecai again refused to bow to him. One of his servants told Hegai that he—Haman, that is—was in a rage."

Esther felt fear clutch her. "And?"

"And they say that Haman had a gallows, higher than any in the land, built to hang Mordecai on."

"Oh, no!" Esther's cry was filled with pain.

"Wait, my lady. Something else happened in the night. Our lord, the king, couldn't sleep, so he finally called Ator to come to his room and read to him one of the scrolls that told the history of his reign. Ator had been asleep, he told me, and was groggy, so he just grabbed the first scroll that came to his hand."

"Is this important?" Esther interrupted, thinking with horror of the gallows which had been erected.

"Terribly important, my lady. The scroll which Ator got by accident was the one which told of the time that Mordecai saved the king's life."

Suhas stopped with a triumphant look, and Esther leaned against the pillows, weak with amazement.

"When the king asked Ator if Mordecai had ever been rewarded, Ator said no, and the king said he would do something about it. He has just sent word that he would like you to join him for breakfast, my lady."

"The king?"

"Yes, my lady. Hurry."

"You should have told me at once," Esther gasped, jumping out of bed.

"But you had to know what had happened during the night, my lady. Maybe the king wants to ask you what he should do for Mordecai. He knows that the gatekeeper is your friend."

"But he mustn't know that Mordecai is my relative," Esther said. "Not yet. Now, quickly, get me dressed."

In only a few minutes, Esther was standing at the king's door, and when she was announced, Ahasuerus turned to her with a wide smile.

"Good morning, my queen," he cried, lifting his scepter. "Come, join me. I was reminded last night of the time your friend, Mordecai, saved my life. I thought you'd like to be here to see what reward I have in mind for him."

"Yes, my lord," she said, wondering what Ahasuerus would say when he learned that Mordecai was soon to be killed by the command of the grand emir.

"As soon as Haman comes," Ahasuerus said, "you'll see what I have in mind."

A voice cried out, "The grand emir to see the king!" and Esther looked up to see Haman coming through the door. His face was glowing with pleasure, and he was rubbing his hands together. It seemed obvious that Haman was thinking with glee of the cruel gibbet he had built and of the man he intended to hang from it.

"Good morning, Haman," the king cried. "I have something to ask you. I need your advice."

"Anything," Haman said eagerly, hurrying toward the throne, "I'll do anything in my power to please my king."

Esther sat very still, her hands shaking so badly that she had to clutch them together in her lap. What would happen when the king announced that he wanted to reward Mordecai, Haman's enemy?

17

Whom the King Wishes to Honor

To Esther's astonishment, Ahasuerus didn't even mention Mordecai's name.

"There's a man," the king began, watching Haman closely, "whom I very much want to honor. I want it to be a very high honor. What do you think I ought to do for him?"

The look of greed and expectation on Haman's face was as easy for Esther to read as the lettering on her precious scrolls. Haman thought the king meant that the honor would be done to him. He pretended to consider the question, but Esther saw the excitement on his face.

"Well, if I were the king . . ." Haman began. Esther

heard an unmistakable longing in his tone. That was exactly what he wanted, she thought. He wanted to be king. Oh, why didn't Ahasuerus recognize the ambition in the man to whom he had given so much power?

"If I were the king," Haman went on, "I'd take one of my robes, a very fine one that I'd worn for some important function, and I'd order one of my own horses, and put the royal crest on it . . ."

His voice hesitated a bit, and Esther saw Ahasuerus's sudden intent look as though he had just become aware of Haman's greed.

"Then," Haman continued, licking his lips, "I'd call one of my highest princes to me. I'd command the prince to put the king's robe on the man to be honored, and I would have the man placed on the king's horse. Finally, I'd have the prince lead the horse through the entire town of Shushan, crying out at every corner that this is the man the king wishes to honor."

Ahasuerus's eyes narrowed, and Esther waited, breathless.

"What a splendid idea!" Ahasuerus said at last. "Only you, my friend, could have come up with such a plan. I will choose you—" He paused briefly, and Haman leaned forward expectantly. "I will choose you," the king repeated, "to lead the horse throughout Shushan. The grand emir himself will put my robe on Mordecai and put him on my own horse, the horse wearing the royal crest."

For the space of several heartbeats, there was absolute silence in the room.

Haman stared at the king. The grand emir's face first grew deathly pale and then flushed until it was almost purple. "Mordecai?" he whispered in a strangled voice.

"Why, yes. The gatekeeper at the south gate," Ahasuerus said casually. "He saved my life by bringing the treachery of Bigthan and Teresh to my attention. He has never been rewarded. Last night, it just so happened that the affair was recalled for me. So—" He spread his hands as though he had explained everything.

Esther repeated the king's words in her head. "Just so happened—" No. None of this was coincidence. When Ator's hand had picked up that particular scroll, Yahweh had guided his fingers.

"Go, then," Ahasuerus said impatiently. "Must I give my orders a second time?"

"No, my lord." Haman bowed his head and stumbled toward the door. Outrage and humiliation were written plainly on his face and in the curve of his bowed shoulders.

"The queen and I look forward to seeing you tonight," Ahasuerus called out and then turned to Esther. "Does it please you that I've dealt so with your friend, the gatekeeper?"

She smiled. "My lord, you are too good. Here, may I serve you? Will you have some bread? A bowl of milk?"

"Both," said Ahasuerus. "I'm starved. Later, when my horse has been returned, I'll go riding, I think. That will hurry the hours until we come to your apartment to dine."

"And I, my lord, will busy myself with preparations," she said. *Not only with the food and entertainment*, she was thinking. *I'll be praying for the words to plead for the lives of the Jews.*

The evening was not as pleasant as the one before it. Haman, try as he might, could not throw off the humiliation of the day. And Ahasuerus acted as though he were tired of sharing his queen's company with anyone, even Haman, his grand emir.

Sensing these things, Esther cut the entertainment short and turned to Ahasuerus.

"Does the king require anything?" she asked.

"Only that you finally state your petition," he said. "I've told you twice now that you may have anything you want, even to half of my kingdom." He laughed. "A man begins to get nervous when a woman won't tell him what she wants."

Esther was very serious. "I do have a petition, my lord. If I have found favor in the sight of the king—"

Ahasuerus interrupted. "You know how I feel about you. Come, tell me what you want."

"If it please the king," Esther said slowly, "I ask that the king give me my life—yes, and the life of my people."

She was aware of Haman's startled stillness and of the king's openmouthed astonishment.

"For we are all to be killed, my lord," she went on. "An edict has gone out which will kill me and all my people. If the edict had only sold us into slavery, my lord, I would not have troubled the king. But the edict calls for our death."

Ahasuerus found his tongue. "Who?" he demanded furiously. "Who would dare do such a dreadful thing?"

Esther's finger pointed to Haman, who suddenly cowered on his couch. "There, my lord," she said without faltering. "There is the man who has condemned to death every Jew who lives in the king's provinces. And I, my lord, among them. For I am the cousin of Mordecai, the Jew. I too am a follower of Yahweh."

Ahasuerus stared in horror from Esther to Haman and back to Esther again. Pushing himself to his feet so abruptly that he toppled his couch to the floor, he flung himself away from the table and plunged through the door that led into the garden. From where she sat, Esther could see the king striding up and down the garden paths, obviously in a state of shock.

After watching Ahasuerus for a minute, Esther turned back to stare at Haman. He tried to meet her eyes, but after only a few seconds, his own dropped.

"My lady," he began.

"Would you speak so humbly to a Jew?" Esther's voice was cold.

"You must listen to me," Haman cried. "I had no idea you were a Jew. Do you think I would have done this to you?"

"Yes." Her reply was clipped.

Haman jumped out of his seat and came toward her. "You've got to believe me," he babbled. "It was only the man, Mordecai. If he had bowed to me as he was supposed to, none of this would have happened."

She stared up into the red, sweating face. "One little man, a gatekeeper, someone who could neither threaten nor hurt you, failed to bow before you. And for this you would kill a whole *nation* of people?" She stopped and asked a painful question. "How did you persuade the king to agree to such a cruel plan?"

Haman was too frightened to be anything but honest. "He didn't know who the Jews were, my lady. He was hardly listening to me that day. I promised him ten thousand talents and I told him he would be saved from treachery. He has grown very cautious about treachery."

"And if Mordecai had not been a Jew," she asked, "would you have sent out such an edict?"

"He would not bow to me," Haman said, stubborn in spite of his fear. "All Jews are stubborn. If Mordecai refused to bow, soon all Jews would do the same."

"Spoken like a true Amalekite!" she cried.

Haman's eyes widened. He threw himself onto the floor, clawing at the couch on which she sat. "Please, my lady," he begged, his voice breaking, "have pity on me."

Esther's voice was brittle. "You've condemned all the children of Yahweh to death. And you expect me to pity you?"

As though to emphasize his need for mercy, Haman cast himself across the foot of the couch. Disgusted and sickened, Esther tried to get up, and there was the thin sound of tearing silk from the corner of her robe imprisoned under Haman's body.

Ahasuerus, coming into the room, saw Esther's face and heard the sound of tearing silk. He lunged at Haman and grabbed him about the throat.

"You dare?" he shouted. "You dare to touch the queen?"

Haman's face went white with despair. A slave, standing by, hearing the king's words, took a cloth and draped it over Haman's head. Everyone in the room knew that, in that moment, Haman's death sentence had been pronounced.

The slave's voice was very loud in the sudden quiet. "There is a gallows, my lord, higher than any in the land. This man, Haman, had it built only last night. He planned to kill Mordecai on it."

The king shrugged, averting his face. "Take him, then," he said tonelessly. "Hang him on his own gibbet."

In a dreadful silence, Haman was led from the room. Esther and Ahasuerus stood alone, looking at each other.

"You should have told me," the king said hoarsely. "You know I would never have allowed the edict to go out if I had known."

"That I was a Jew? Uncle Mordecai forbade me to tell."

"But what now? A royal edict, once issued, cannot be reversed! There is still an edict that all the Jews shall die on the thirteenth of Adar." He stared into her face. "How shall I save my beloved and her people?"

She put out her hand and took the king's hand to lead him to the couch. "Sit here, my lord," she begged, suddenly sure of what to say and equally sure that the king would listen to her.

"My God has given me a plan," she said. "A second edict can be issued. This one will give the Jews the right to arm themselves against the soldiers on the thirteenth of Adar. The Jews know how to protect themselves, my lord, if they are given the right to fight."

Ahasuerus's face brightened. "A good idea. We can send our poorest soldiers against the Jews, and the Jews will be free to use swords, knives—"

"Yes, my lord!" Esther concurred. Then she stopped,

puzzled. "But what about me? And my Uncle Mordecai? He is a scholar, and I am a woman. We can't use swords."

Ahasuerus thought for a minute and then began to smile. "I'm in need of a grand emir, you know," he said at last. "One I can trust completely. Would this Mordecai be able to serve me, do you think?"

"Oh, my lord!" Her eyes were shining. "He's wise and clever and completely honest. He's—"

The king interrupted. "It sounds as though you think him the greatest man in all the world."

"Oh, no, my lord. *You* are the greatest man," she said simply.

Ahasuerus's arms went around her and drew her close to him. "You are my queen," he said, "and anyone who would harm you must contend with me first."

Her heart was singing. *I am*, she thought gratefully, *the most blessed of women.*

"And now," Ahasuerus said, "shall we send a message to your Uncle Mordecai? Let us tell him that because Esther was brave enough to petition me, the Jews will not perish. And let us tell him that from this day on, Haman's house and all his possessions belong to Mordecai, who once was the keeper of the gate."

Her eyes were dancing. "Thank you, my lord. I know you will receive all Mordecai's devotion and loyalty."

"And yours?" Ahasuerus asked very softly, as though he were just an ordinary man and not a king who could command that he be loved.

"Oh, yes, my lord! Always!" she promised and bent to kiss his hand.

To her astonishment, he pulled his hand away. "No,"

he said, almost harshly. "Other people bend to kiss my hand, but not you. You are my wife, and I love you."

She looked into his eyes, hardly daring to believe what he was saying.

"And not only because you're beautiful," Ahasuerus added with a smile of understanding, "but because you are what you are: brave, and wise, and good."

He touched his lips to hers, and his kiss was sweet and warm and filled with the promise of a bright tomorrow.